Coming Out Happy
(Life Doesn't Have To Suck)

Dani Max

Copyright © 2017 Dani Max
All rights reserved.
No part of this book may be reproduced, stored in a retrieval
system, or transmitted by any means, electronic, mechanical,
photocopy, recording, or otherwise, without
written permission from the author.
ISBN: 1974672190
ISBN 13: 9781974672196

Printed in the United States of America

Cover photo by Alyssa Colletti
Editing by Jessica Vineyard, Red Letter Editing, LLC www.redletterediting.com

Dani Max
127 N Broadway
Hicksville, NY 11801
DaniMaxWorldWide.com

Other books by Dani Max
To The Maxx! : A Teen's Perspective on How Any Teen Can Create Their Ultimate Career and Life
(Recommended by Brian Tracy)

Table of Contents

Acknowledgments	v
Prologue: My Story	vii
Introduction	xxxi
Lesson 1 Acknowledge	1
Lesson 2 Accept	5
Lesson 3 Allow	13
Lesson 4 Adventure	23
Lesson 5 Activate	30
Epilogue	35
About the Author	38

Acknowledgments

A VERY SPECIAL thank you to my family for their unconditional love. Thank you to my friends for being the ultimate support system, especially when I needed them the most. A huge thank you to my supporters. The many ways you show your love inspires me more than you can imagine. I also want to thank the people who've hurt me. I've learned so much from you, and you've been my greatest teachers. Lastly, I want to thank you for reading this book. I hope it makes you see the possibilities about how beautiful life can be, and that it doesn't have to suck. Much love. You got this!

Prologue: My Story

IF YOU GO to any of my social media, there's a good chance I'm smiling really hard in my most recent picture. If you don't know who I am at all, I will look like any other brown-haired, green-eyed, five-feet-tall girl who's posing for a picture. But the girl in that picture worked hard for that smile . . . I earned that smile. You see, it's not just a grin, it's something real, and I'm bursting with true happiness.

As I write this, I am a twenty-two-year-old college graduate from Long Island, New York. I am also a singer/songwriter and have released songs to major platforms such as iTunes and Spotify. I'm a sister, a daughter, and may I say, a very good friend. I wake up every day feeling grateful and excited about life and my future, and it shows in everything I do. I'm goofy and a little shy when you first meet me, but I have a huge, giving heart. I live every single day to the fullest, with hopes of inspiring the world with what I've learned about life at a young age.

I am this way because of the change in mindset I had when I hit complete rock bottom at twenty years old. I transformed myself from being depressed, insecure, and feeling unworthy into someone I am extremely proud to be today. I am young and imperfect because I'm human, and I don't pretend to be anything else. Over these last two years, I have learned how to love and accept myself, and I finally know what I'm worth as a whole, beautiful human being. Man, facing the demons in my head I thought I would never be able to heal from was really hard work.

If you don't know my story of how I got to be a confident young woman, you may ask how someone who's smiling so hard can teach lessons learned from being sad, angry, and hurt. Well, my happiness and self-love are newly found.

Here's the story of how I *created* them, and in the upcoming chapters, I'm going to show you how you can create happiness and self-love, too.

Up until I was about eleven years old, I didn't think much about what people thought of me because I didn't understand what judgment even was. I played sports, dressed in my own style, and hung out with whoever I wanted to. I was always a tomboy who was quiet and kind; tiny in stature but fierce in playing sports. I was unaware that people had their own interpretation of others they came in contact with. At the time, I didn't really judge anyone, and I especially didn't judge myself; I just was who I was. I did think girls were pretty, though, and that was the only judgment I made.

In elementary school there was this girl I bonded with, and I told my mom I made a new friend. After realizing that I wanted to kiss this girl, I then told my mom I thought I was gay. I thought I could be open about it with my mom, who loved her children inside and out, for better or for worse. As I sat her down to tell her my feelings, she was confused about what brought this up for me. I'll never forget it; she said, "Dan, would you rather kiss a boy or a girl?" I took a moment to question myself, then responded with "I guess . . . a boy." I was brought up watching Disney movies with princesses and princes, so even though my gut told me who I had feelings for, my mind told me that I should be kissing a boy instead. My mom and I talked about how I was young and it was okay to find girls attractive, but she didn't realize that this was my way of "coming out," and she dismissed my feelings. I guess she thought I was too young to really understand them. I love my mom, but this conversation made me question my first instinct, and it made me think that I didn't actually like girls. After our talk, I suppressed my feelings, and weirdly enough, I almost forgot about them until I was about sixteen years old.

At the middle school I entered, three different elementary schools fed into one big school, which meant meeting all new people. I was that quiet girl who went to school, played sports, and hung out with the family. I started to notice that I was gaining weight, and even though I was always active as a kid, I did have a love for great food.

Typically, in middle school there are always those boys who think they're so cool and attractive and can speak to anyone as they please. I never associated

Coming Out Happy (Life Doesn't Have to Suck)

myself with people like that, but I was surrounded by them every day. I remember once when I was in seventh grade, we had a test to take in math class one day. The classroom was set up in narrow rows, so if you wanted to walk to the front of the classroom, it could be a tight squeeze depending on your size. When I finished my test, I stood up and started walking toward the teacher to hand in my test. At the same time, one of those typical middle school boys was returning to his seat in the same row as me, so we had to pass each other. I had my head down and casually walked to the front when he said, "Move, fat ass." I couldn't believe that people spoke like that, and it hurt me to my core because those hurtful words were targeted at me. I felt ashamed and embarrassed. I handed in my test, let him pass, broke down, and kept to myself the rest of the day. I was now a notch lower in confidence, and I was only twelve years old.

Eighth grade was another confusing year. I became very close with a friend who lived nearby. We were so different from one another, but we were attached at the hip. It was the first time I let someone into my life. I felt like I could depend on her and called her my best friend. She was the girl who everyone loved, every boy swooned over, and I was her sidekick. I began to question myself, asking, "Am I not good enough or pretty enough?" As I spent more time with her, I started noticing that she took advantage of me and would always put me down. I let it continue because she was the closest person I had in my life and I told her everything. I was dependent and had latched onto someone who wasn't a good friend at all. I started comparing myself to her, which led to my being upset and taking it out on myself in many unhealthy ways. I felt bad about myself, and that's why I let the friendship continue for as long as it did. I didn't feel worthy of a friend who would treat me the way a real friend should be treated. Eventually I realized it was a toxic friendship.

I was at a point in my life where girls started to like boys, and that was confusing for me. I never was attracted to boys as much as the other girls were, but I felt pressured because everyone seemed to be boy obsessed. I had an overpowering friend, a very low self-esteem, and was confused about my nonexistent love life. I started to talk to boys, but my insecure mind told me that I wasn't girly or pretty enough. I went for boys who weren't nice or respectful and who were the typical young cocky kid.

IX

Dani Max

I hit my first rock bottom at the age of thirteen after doing things I wasn't proud of with a boy who took advantage of my naïve mind. The worst part about the whole thing was that I felt like there was no one there to support me when I fell. I felt too embarrassed telling anyone, including my close-knit family, about my regrettable decisions. In the back of my mind I couldn't help but blame this girl for making me feel like I wasn't good enough. But it wasn't her fault; I let her make me feel this way because I felt bad about myself. I let the boy take advantage of me even as I blamed him for his actions.

I learned from those experiences. I eventually felt ashamed that I had stooped so low because I didn't feel good about myself. I learned that year that I deserved better in friendships and that I wasn't into boys as much as I'd hoped. But even though I realized those things, I felt so lost. I was walking around with my head down in school and becoming even more shy and insecure than I was before. Every day when I came home from school, I went into my room, shut off the lights, and slept for the rest of the day, just hoping time would pass and I'd feel better. I didn't want to be seen, and I started gaining an insane amount of weight because of it. I was dead inside, and my actions showed that I had given up on life. At just fourteen years old, I had my first taste of being depressed and feeling betrayed, damaged, and purely heartbroken.

After that painful school year ended, my friend transferred schools and I felt a sudden weight off my shoulders. But transitioning to high school is usually a rough time for most. As a tiny freshman, I walked around the halls like I didn't belong anywhere. I had no idea who I was, what I wanted, and now I had no friends. I carried around this chip on my shoulder from my past—an anger I'll never forget—and I took it out on my family, who never deserved it. I wasn't nice to anyone, and I walked around angry at the world.

Only two things made me happy: music and tennis. I had been playing tennis ever since I was a kid, and that year I worked hard to finally make it onto the varsity team. Tennis became a huge part of my life. It helped me get my anger out and become more social, even when I didn't want to be; in some way, it saved me.

I excelled on the court but still felt like a failure as a person. I couldn't let go or forgive myself for the mistakes I had made that had built up over the last few

Coming Out Happy (Life Doesn't Have to Suck)

years. My anger and resentment showed up in every aspect of my life. Later, in my twenties, I learned that there are no mistakes, only lessons.

In my freshman year of high school, I met my best friends, who I am still close with to this day. What blessings best friends can be. We just clicked. We understood each other during a rough time in our lives. I had never before had friendships that felt right with people I could really relate to. Of course we had our fights (and still have them), but we developed a real bond that I will never forget. I now had true friends, and with their help, I no longer felt like staying in bed anymore. Life was still messy, but having good friends made me feel a little better. Although my mind still wasn't right, I was taking a step in the right direction, and being surrounded by the right people helped.

Sophomore year rolled around, and I was still insecure Dani, judging my mind and body. But now I wanted to figure out another piece of the puzzle: what was love, and could I find it? I was ready to date or be in a relationship, even though I wasn't sure what that really meant. I had spent my freshman year not talking to any boys after my traumatic experience, never questioning or thinking deeper about why I wasn't actually interested, but I wanted to feel *something*. I thought maybe it was just the boys in my school, so I turned to social media to meet someone and came across a guy I thought was cute. We had mutual friends, and it turned out that he lived in the same town and our families knew of each other, so I decided to message him to see if he'd message me back. He immediately responded, which made me happy. I didn't really know how I felt about him, but he was a good-looking kid, respectful, and he seemed super nice, so I kept it going. He asked me on a date, something I had never had before, but I got the courage to say yes. We met up at a local bowling alley and really had a lot of fun.

One date led to another, and then he asked me to be his girlfriend. I didn't know why he wanted to be with me because I didn't see any good qualities in myself, but finally being able to tell my confused self and the world that I had a boyfriend put me at ease. He told me I was beautiful, and although I never really believed it, I gave the relationship a shot and gave him my heart. After a few months of dating, I just couldn't see myself getting physical with him, and he told me that he couldn't see us working out if that was the case. We broke up, and

XI

I cried to my mom openly about my second feeling of heartbreak. I was so angry with myself; I didn't know why I didn't want to move forward with him. But we both respected my decision, and we decided we just weren't right for each other. Maybe I was too insecure, maybe I was too immature, or maybe (as I figured out later on) I just wasn't attracted to boys. Exploring my sexuality wasn't even anything I considered, so I moved on and spent time alone, because that's what I was used to anyway.

That same year, music and singing helped me feel better the same way tennis did. I never sang in front of crowds, but when I sang, the feelings I felt were indescribable. In the moments when I was totally engulfed in music, I wasn't thinking about my insecurities, my doubts, or my sadness. I sang loudly, danced, and felt empowered—even if it was only in front of my mirror. My family had always told me I was talented, and that was the one compliment I believed. The confidence I was starting to feel made me want to take it further than just singing in the shower, so I started making cover songs on YouTube. I picked a few songs that I knew by heart, recorded them on my computer, and clicked "Upload." I didn't know what the world would think of my voice, but I knew I wanted to share it. I showed my friends and eventually posted the videos on my Facebook page. They somehow made their way to the rude boys from my high school, who left comments making fun of something that took a lot for me to share. I felt defeated, uncomfortable, and embarrassed. Over and over again in my life I felt the world judging me and let it affect my actions. I was so upset that I took the videos down and gave up on posting anything about my music.

Junior year came around, and I was still playing tennis, still hanging out with my friends, still going to school with my head down in a crowded place. I was still gaining weight, still being insanely insecure about my every move, but now it was time to look at colleges, the next step in my life. It was time to figure out more about the *who* of Dani—a career. This was another huge mystery I didn't have an answer for, but here's a little bit of my background, which definitely shaped my decisions.

Both of my parents are entrepreneurs, and thinking out of the box was a mindset I always carried with me. My mom went to school for journalism, and when she realized it wasn't for her, she went back to school, then built a health, lifestyle, and empowerment business for women. She started seeing clients, writing books, creating products and programs, and sharing her message on TV and radio and by speaking to audiences all around the country. Her goal was to help people create their best mindset and healthiest self, and her past helped her learn exactly what to teach others.

My mom was so passionate about helping people . . . but who listens to their mom, right? Funny how I never cared to understand anything about her business and gained weight despite all of her efforts to try to help me. While her ideas about life are exactly what I love talking about now, back then I didn't *want* to listen. I wasn't *ready* to understand anything about happiness, life, or having a choice. I was rebelling against *everything* she did and taught—until it all made perfect sense. At the time, I didn't realize that what I would eventually be doing in my own career was going to be so similar to what my mom taught, because I didn't feel like I had overcome anything worth teaching at my age. When I looked at her career, I saw that her happiness didn't come just from how much money she made but through her heart and desire to help and impact others. But since I thought I didn't have any passions, experiences, or talents like my mom did, I looked instead to my dad, and I thought that business would be what would make me and my family proud.

My dad is a real estate broker who started his company with two people on his team and grew it to an office with more than thirty people. He is a great salesman, persuasive yet lovable, and he knew right out of college that business was right for him. Success in business is what he prided himself on, and ever since I was little, I listened to how important thinking differently was in order for success to happen. Money played a huge role in his life, and to him having money meant success. I saw my dad work extremely hard to create his own company and knew that although money doesn't buy happiness, it makes life a lot easier. Since my dad made money and loved what he did, I was driven to find a career path where I could do the same. I wasn't thinking about helping people, I was thinking about making money, and going into business seemed like the best way to do it. I started to look at colleges with good entrepreneurship programs.

Near the end of my junior year, when people were applying to schools and really figuring out their next steps, my mom heard of a beautiful college that was highly recommended by business professionals and entrepreneurs. I did my research and liked what I saw, so we booked a flight to North Carolina. I didn't feel mentally ready to go to college at all, but I went with my mom, looked around, and thought that if I had to get out of my comfort zone, at least this place was pretty. I didn't make any decisions but applied to a few schools that summer.

Senior year . . . wow. I finally made it to the last year of being in a place I was mentally done with. I was so ready to finish high school and get away from everything I had ever known. Senior year also meant prom, activities, and of course, more self-discovery. I had applied to the colleges I wanted to, I had my friends, and everything was working out. But another year meant more time to figure out who I was and what I wanted.

On the first day of classes we were getting settled in, figuring out where we wanted to sit, and seeing if our friends had the same classes. I found one of my friends who had a class with me, and we sat together in the back. We were laughing about nonsense, and this blonde-haired athletic girl walked in and went to the front to take a seat. My heart stopped for a minute, I got really nervous, and my face—well, I was blushing. I didn't know who she was, but it turned out she had transferred to my school the previous year.

As class started, we were all introducing ourselves to the people around us, but she and I didn't speak to each other. There was a rumor going around that she was openly gay. I had heard this, and if it was true, I wondered what that was like for her. I thought that going to a new school must have been hard enough, but being open about something like that must have made it much harder. There were only a few openly gay guys in my school, and they were judged and bullied, but never any lesbians that I knew about—or at least any that caught my eye like she did.

After a few weeks, I was in a group with her and a few others who I was friendly with. We started talking, and since she was semi-new to the school and was as quiet as I was, I asked where she was from. She responded with the name of a town that I used to be rivals with in tennis, so I asked her if she knew a girl who I knew on their team. She gave me a weird look, put her head down, and said, "Yeah, I know her. That's my ex-girlfriend." I realized a couple of things in that moment: the rumors about her were true, and I was going to have something to deal with because I wanted to know so much about what that was like for her. A girlfriend? In high school? I never even considered anything like that, but I knew that the interest I had in her and her experiences were way deeper than just being curious.

I thought she was beautiful and mysterious, so I needed to know more about this lifestyle she lived. We started joking with each other during class, and that led to walking down the hallways together. I couldn't stop thinking about her, and I didn't know why.

I wanted to be close to her, so I told her that if she was ever free, we should hang out. She was skeptical at first, confused about my intentions, but told me to hang out with her while she was at work at a local ice cream shop. I went in one day, and we just talked for hours. She told me about her past, what her girlfriend was like, and I listened intently to every word she said. We got to really know each other, but we never told each other how we felt about this blooming new friendship we had or about my sexuality in general.

As we gained each other's trust, she became more comfortable speaking openly with me. One day, after running errands together, she told me she liked me as more than a friend. I felt that feeling of having a crush in my heart, in my soul, and I'd never had a girl tell me that before, so I wasn't sure how to respond. I didn't say anything back, because even though my first instinct the day I met her was that I liked her, the fear of judgement held me back from really figuring out my feelings for her. She left to go home, and I got in my car for a trip in my own thoughts. I knew that if I didn't figure out my feelings for her, I'd lose her, but I was truly petrified.

After this happened, we still hung out, but I didn't share the fears I was battling against this whole new world I so badly wanted to discover. There were so many what-ifs, so much judgment I might face, so I blocked out the one perfect opportunity to talk about it.

A few weeks went by, and I still never said how I felt, even though I knew she knew. Then one day she told me she wanted to talk to me. She looked into my eyes and told me, "My best friend from my old town told me she was in love with me. I'm going to start dating her, and I wanted to tell you." I felt sick. I wondered if I had just been honest with myself, felt my fear, and went for it anyway, would things be different? I was so sad, but I understood that she wanted someone who was open and owned their feelings. At the time, that just wasn't who I was. I was so angry with myself but wasn't ready to take the next step.

After she told me that she was no longer available, something started to change in my brain. At this point, I needed to be aware of my thoughts, because what I had been doing, denying my feelings and being too afraid to experiment, had been keeping me from discovering my true self. I started to really question what I wanted and who I wanted to be. This girl was the first friend I had who introduced me to the idea of being openly gay, and it made me see that it was really possible, when I was ready. Having feelings for her were no longer an option, so I did a lot of self-reflecting for a few weeks. I knew that I wasn't content with a few things in my life—my confused sexuality as well as my body. Because I wasn't focusing on her anymore, now was the time to really work on myself, and I thought losing some weight would be a good start at making myself happy.

I decided to finally stop rebelling against my mom and the health and lifestyle coach she is. I asked her how to lose weight, and she gave me a talk in eating healthy and exercising. I decided to try it to see if it worked, and after a week of healthier eating and going to the gym, I lost a few pounds. I felt great and kept going with it because I kept seeing results every single day. As I started to lose weight, I became more confident, not because of the way I looked, but because of how I felt doing something to help myself. For years, the extra weight made me insecure, but when I saw that I was able to take this part of my life into my own hands, I felt empowered and didn't give up. I started to believe in myself and saw that when I put my mind toward something, I could achieve it. This was when I started to understand what loving myself was.

As I was finally doing something positive for myself, I took the time to be in my own head, which was terrifying. I was ready to face one of my biggest struggles. Instead of fully denying the obvious feelings I was having, I started to say to myself, "I liked her. I think I like girls, but I'm scared." No one told me I needed to figure out who I wanted to be with besides myself. It made me upset that at seventeen years old I wasn't certain about my sexuality, but I wish someone had told me that I needed to trust the process. I wish I knew that everything would end up okay in the end and I would figure myself out and that there was no need to worry. But of course, I was a mess back then. I felt everything bubble up inside me, and my heart hurt so bad. But saying to myself that I liked girls was progress, and I was proud to finally stop denying it. This was the start of accepting my feelings and being okay with the things I couldn't change.

Because I still trusted that girl, I told her I wanted to talk to her about something that was stressing me out. We went to talk after school one day, and I took the time I needed to breathe before speaking. My mind was going in a million different directions, and I was shaking and basically felt like I couldn't breathe. I told her, "Please don't tell anyone . . . please. I'm bisexual, and I needed to tell someone." That moment, the first time I had EVER said anything out loud besides "Yes, I'm straight," was extremely nerve-wracking yet empowering. I said it, it was out to one person, and that was all I needed to start my journey of accepting myself. Back then, I said I was bisexual because I still wasn't certain of my own feelings, but I wanted to label it as something so I could try to understand it in some way. My coming out to her wasn't for her as much as it was for me, and I felt a weight lifted from my shoulders. I was able to say those words out loud to another human being, which I never imagined myself doing, but I found the courage to be true to myself. She told me that she wouldn't tell anyone, but I was still stuck in my own head, wondering what would happen if it ever got out to the kids at my school. We started to part ways a bit after this, because I think she may have been angry that I hadn't made this discovery earlier, and I was still heartbroken that she was now happy with someone else. I wondered what the next step would be in this confusing time for me.

As I continued through my senior year of high school, I began to think it was time. It was time to make myself happy and not hide everything I was struggling with, so I thought of who I wanted to share these new thoughts with and started with my family. My family and I have the dynamic where we can be open with our feelings, but no one forces us to talk if we don't want to say anything. I never spoke to my family much with my struggles *at all* before coming out, even though they would have always been there for me no matter what.

One day, before tennis had started, I was driving with one of my brothers, who I joke around a lot with and is close to me in age. I mentioned to him that I had something to share. I said that I liked the girl from school, who he knew of, and that I thought I liked both boys and girls. He didn't know if I was being serious, and his face was filled with confusion. He didn't know what to say, so he didn't really say anything, and the conversation was over. It just wasn't as big of a deal to him as I thought it would be. Even though I know he loves and accepts me, to this day he knows I wasn't too happy with his minimal response.

I started to see that coming out was hard for me because I latched onto what I thought the other person's reaction would be instead of realizing that coming out was purely for me. I told my brother not to tell anyone, and he agreed, but he said to tell Mom and Dad. My own parents . . . what would they think of their first born having this kind of secret to share? I was so scared, even though they are open and loving people. I couldn't stop questioning what it would be like after coming out to them.

Two days later, I built up the courage. As I was driving with my dad, I told him to play 21 Questions with me. Somehow we ended up on the topic of dating, and he asked me if I had a boyfriend. I responded with a laugh and a no, and then he asked "a girlfriend?" I froze. I knew that I had been given the opportunity to finally say it, and I felt like it was now or never. I started to cry and said, "Not exactly." He had no idea why I was crying, but I continued with, "I think I'm gay, Dad." I was not confused anymore. As I started to come out to more and more people, I knew that I would be judged no matter what I said or how I felt, so I may as well be completely honest. We talked for a bit, and he reminded me that no matter who I loved, I would always be his tomboy daughter who he would never judge. He said, "I think it's time to go home and tell Mom."

We got home, and I was puffy-eyed from balling my eyes out just minutes before. My mom got into the back seat, not knowing what had happened to me. I was a mess, and I started to cry again. It took me a bit to stop and say the words. "I'm gay, Mom." I was sitting in the front seat looking straight ahead. I didn't look her in the eyes when I said it because I was still so afraid. She leaned up to me and said that it didn't matter at all, she would always love me, and the most important thing was that I was happy. I cried from happiness and relief, and then my parents proceeded to ask me questions: "Are you sure? Do you think this is just a phase? You know this is a harder road to take in life, right?" They were asking out of curiosity, and they just wanted me to be sure of how I felt. I knew that they would never try to change how I felt and that they just wanted me to be happy with myself, but I knew deep down that this wasn't something that would change, and I was at a place where I didn't question my feelings. I felt how I felt and was happy to be sharing it with my parents. After coming out to my parents and one of my brothers, I felt closer to them than I ever had before. I felt less stressed and calmer in my mind, and I needed that.

During the end of senior year, I was accepted to the college in North Carolina that I wanted and made the decision to commit, despite all my fears of being far away and the huge change that was bound to happen anyway. I was worried about what coming out to new people would be like, because I hadn't even done it with my closest friends at high school, but knew there would be a time and a place for both of those things to happen.

I had worked incredibly hard over the last few months to lose forty pounds, which made me so proud. Losing weight and looking better hit me so fast that I wasn't really sure how to feel about my new look, but everyone noticed the change I had made. People were noticing me who had never looked at me before, and I started to gain confidence, which was new to me. I felt better than I had ever felt in my entire life. But my new exterior look didn't cure the anxiety I was having about the unknown that was coming—college and coming out. I was looking great but still feeling unhappy, but at least now I was taking small steps toward becoming happier.

The last month of school was filled with prom and goodbyes. I knew that I'd never get those moments back, so I made the most of it and went to prom with a guy friend and had a blast with my best friends. Graduation day finally rolled around, and everyone had their caps and gowns on and tears were rolling down their faces. I, on the other hand, wanted to run off that stage and out of that school as fast as I could. My best friends and I saw each other before the ceremony, and we knew nothing would break our friendships after graduating.

My entire class and their families filled up the high school auditorium, and the ceremony began. I got through it; I'm not sure how I survived, but I was so happy because I started to see the light within myself. I received my certificate, smiled, and left with my family, overwhelmed with emotions. My high school years were ones I would always remember, and they were finally behind me. I learned so much about myself during those seventeen years, but it was time to start a new journey, going to college at High Point University.

I was seventeen, scared, and wasn't ready for college, yet I had no choice. I packed up everything I owned to take with me. I had chosen to do a summer program with a hundred other incoming freshmen so I could get a head start on classes, meet new people, and hopefully use the extra time to get comfortable before school officially started. As an introvert, I was terrified at the idea of having to make new friends, but I knew that life was better with friends, so I decided to give it all a try.

On the first day of creating my new life, I set up my dorm and met my roommate, who was very nice. We actually had the same first name. We spent a couple of hours unpacking our clothes and talking to each other about high school and what this new place was going to be like for us. At least we had each other, we thought. All you need is to start with one friend to give you the confidence to go out and make another friend and another friend after that. Once I set up my part of the room, I went outside to meet more people.

Looking back on it now, I wish I had stayed in my room that day. The people I met when I left my room changed my life forever, but they also taught me lessons I now share with others. I came across a few people who seemed friendly and wanted to talk. We were so different from each other, but we bonded over the fact that we were all in the same boat: we didn't know anyone, and we were nervous. After spending an hour together, we added a couple more friends into this new little group we had just created.

The summer program was only a month long, but my bond with these new people happened faster than anything I was used to in high school. Maybe it's because when you're in college, you're managing your own time, your own life, and you're in unfamiliar surroundings—and your mom doesn't need you to come home. My new friends wanted to spend all of our time together, and it was great for a while. Little did I know the effect these people were to have on me, and not in a good way. Within the first week I had a solid group of friends that I did my daily activities with. Seems great, right? But during that first week, I latched onto people who were overly involved with drugs and alcohol and were severely struggling in their own heads. My new friends were a mess, and it was scary and unfamiliar to be around their behavior.

I had decided in high school not to drink, but this was college, and I wanted to try it, so I drank a little bit on that first weekend. I didn't know what it would be like to be drunk, and since my friends knew I was new to it, they looked out for me.

I didn't regret my decision to drink, but I did start to re-evaluate my new friendships after I started seeing how constantly careless they were about themselves. It's completely normal to have those nights where you drink a lot or party too hard, but these people never stopped, and it just wasn't something I was interested in. But I had no other friends, and everyone else in the program had already made their friend groups, so I stayed in mine. I didn't know it was okay to switch friend groups if I didn't feel I was in the right one; I just accepted that these were my new friends. Over the course of that month, I became more familiar with the campus and the people around me. I felt hopeful about what the next four years would be like, even if I wasn't into partying as much as my friends were.

The month of dipping my toe in the water of college was over, and it was time to officially start my freshman year. I learned a lot during those few weeks but felt totally behind on acting like a "real" college kid. I went home for two weeks before I returned for the full semester. I kept in touch with my friends from the program, and we looked forward to seeing each other again.

I prepared myself in a few ways before I went back to college. I came out to my friends from home and figured out the new person I wanted to be as a fresh eighteen-year-old college student. My best friends from home have always been open-minded New Yorkers, but for some reason I was still nervous to tell people who I'd been so close with. We sat in the car one day before eating dinner (seems to be my favorite place to come out). I started crying as usual and officially told them that I was gay. They laughed and told me that I shouldn't be crying and that it wasn't too much of a surprise to them, and they would always accept their homie.

Next step: my new look and vibe that I wanted to give off, as I was no longer a high school kid. I was confident with my new weight, and I'd been working out all summer, so I ditched my old style and started wearing more athletic clothes. I felt more like myself, and that felt really good. As I was coming out to more people, I started to understand myself more and started to see that I could be whoever I wanted to be, which meant I didn't have to dress girly if that wasn't who I was. I said my goodbyes to my best friends, and we all went away to college, not sure who we would come back as the next time we'd get together for break.

My first days of college weren't as scary as it probably was for others. I had a few friends, I knew my way around campus, and I felt good. After moving into my new room and doing all of the orientation activities, I met up with my college friends, and we picked up right where we had left off. Classes began, and so did my daily routine. I joined a few clubs, such as tennis, and along with some friends, I even founded a business fraternity on campus. I had the confidence of a great college kid, but something felt wrong. Every day, my new friends were doing something reckless or illegal. On top of that, I was spending my time with people who had really unhealthy habits, thoughts, and behaviors, which affected me. They ate lots of fast food, and before I knew it, I was joining them. I was eating poorly and drinking, and I lost myself again. Where was the girl I was finally proud of? I started to feel weak around these people. They say you are who you surround yourself with, and it's true. I started gaining back every pound I'd lost, and it felt horrible.

Halfway into this terrible first year, I caught pneumonia, and things went from bad to worse. Now I was extremely sick, I was in the hospital, and I had awful habits and awful friends. During this time I also came out to these friends, and half of them decided that our friendship wasn't in their best interest. So now I was left with half of my friends, a really bad sickness, and I felt bad about everything. I went home for Thanksgiving break and tried to heal mentally and physically. I knew I'd lost a few friends who weren't great to begin with, but at least I wasn't sick anymore. Being home, I saw how my healthy habits were slipping, but I ignored it because this was the new life I thought I wanted.

Little did I know that the next two years would be the lowest of my entire life. I lost all motivation to be healthy and started to be mentally abused by my "friends." I once again had no confidence and no self-esteem, and I began taking it out myself, my friends from home, and even my family. I pushed away people

Coming Out Happy (Life Doesn't Have to Suck)

who really cared about me for people who treated me like garbage. I never said no to these people or stood up for myself. I completely lost myself. I was numb. I forgot who I was and became a person I didn't even recognize.

Because I had lost motivation to be healthy physically, mentally, and emotionally, I stopped caring about everything. I also stopped coming out to people and kept it a secret again. I rarely talked to anyone else besides these new people, and I wasn't comfortable trying to make new friends. I gained weight faster than I ever had before, gaining back the forty pounds I had lost, plus an extra twenty pounds. I was letting myself get taken advantage of by my friends, and they knew I'd never do anything to stop it. I was being abused not because I couldn't stop it, but because for some reason, I just didn't. I trusted them. I felt like I didn't even deserve good friends at this point. I saw how they were destroying their lives, and I didn't even care that I was going down with them. I stopped caring about myself, my schoolwork, and my life. I let these friends call me names, ignore me as they pleased, and treat me in ways no real friend ever would.

Freshman year turned into sophomore year and then junior year with the same exact pattern of letting these people control me and make me feel bad about everything I did. I developed a hatred for myself as well as a huge resentment toward them. Years later I learned that no one can control you without your permission, and I also learned that "hurt people hurt people." That's exactly what had happened.

During my sophomore year, my family asked why I allowed these people to hurt me so bad. My only response was that I cared about them so much and I thought they cared back. But if someone cares about you, they don't hurt you, they want the best for you. These people dragged me down to a point where not only did I hate myself, but I started to hate the world. I felt like a victim to it, powerless, careless about everything, and I couldn't stop crying every single day. By junior year, all I had were terrible friends, a body I was miserable with, and a secret I didn't feel safe to share, even though I remembered the feeling of freedom when I had come out to my friends and family in the past. I felt trapped, alone, stuck, miserable, frustrated, angry, and numb—all at the same time.

My biggest fear was to be so miserable that I didn't even want to live, yet that's what I felt like because of what I allowed and put up with. When people asked me in my junior year why I was friends with these people, I didn't even have an answer. My family saw how hard I was struggling inside and how much I was hurting. They wanted so much to help, but they couldn't. No one can help you if you don't want help, and during that time, I was so dependent on these "friends" and so comfortable with feeling bad that I didn't know how to get out of it.

I had no idea how I got to my absolute lowest. but one day it hit me—I couldn't stay like this another day. This wasn't the life I wanted to live anymore, and this negative person wasn't anything like the person I wanted to be.

At twenty years old, and at my lowest point in life, a powerful force from deep within became obvious; I needed to let go of all the negativity or I'd never survive, let alone create a life I wanted. I was sick of being sad, sick of crying, and sick of who I'd become. I spoke to my family and told them that I was scared to let go of my friends because I had no one else. They assured me that I would find other people to hang out with but that I'd never find them if I stayed friends with this destructive group. I was afraid to be alone, but it was hurting me more to be around people who constantly tore me down and had me question myself. I also had so much extra weight on me from all of the drinking and eating, and I didn't know where to start. I felt so confused and lost, but something guided me and gave me hope to start being happy again—whatever that meant. A tiny flicker within turned into a fire, which helped me take care of myself again, something I had given up on years before. During the fall of my junior year, I made the best decision of my life: to take back control and find my happiness.

I knew that figuring out how to love myself again wouldn't be easy, but it would lead to getting my life back. I went into my bedroom, sobbing at the mess I had made of myself over the years, and went into my bathroom. I looked deeply into my own eyes in the mirror and felt every single emotion tower over me: guilt, fear of the future, fear of everything, and lots of anger. As I stared at my reflection and cried over the sink, I yelled at myself, "*I love you, you're beautiful, and you are incredible!*" I needed to say it because I had lost all of the love I had ever given to myself. When I said it, I didn't truly love myself, but it was a start; it was the best thing I could have ever said out loud. I made a promise that I would do this every day with the goal of feeling better and with the hope that one day I'd believe my own words. It didn't happen overnight, but every time I did this new thing, I felt cared about and felt more and more love surround me. I evaluated what I needed to do to make my mind clear. I realized I needed to ditch my toxic food habit as well as my toxic friends. I wanted to start with letting go of these people; I knew it had to be done in order to get better. My family supported me every step of the way and gave me the courage I needed to tell my friends that I no longer wanted to be friends. It was terrifying, but I was finally ready.

While I was at home for break, my college friends started to notice that I wasn't contacting them, and they eventually asked me what was wrong. Our friendship wasn't doing any good for any of us, and this was my opportunity to do something I couldn't have imagined doing before: letting go and moving on. I called them, and although I didn't explain every detail of how they made me feel, I said that I needed time away from them. That phone call represented the first time I stood up for myself. It was hard, but I was finally taking action. I wanted to be mature about it, and my intention was to separate on a kind note. They fought back, but I think they understood that I needed to get back to the happier version of who I had been three years before. The moment I hung up, I felt free, yet terrified of the unknown. My mind was still cluttered, but I believed that dropping what was hurting me would help me see more clearly. I went back to school, still nervous about my future, but with faith in myself to create the strong-minded young woman I always knew I was and would be again.

The next step in helping myself was getting back to being physically healthy. I had lost forty pounds four years before, so although this was going to be really hard, I knew how to do it. I dreaded every minute of exchanging fast food and alcohol for healthy salads and going to the gym, but it didn't stop me.

I wasn't under anyone's control anymore. I branched out and started to talk to new people. I made friends wherever I went and became closer with people I knew from classes and clubs. This time, they were kind, hardworking people and saw bright futures for themselves. I created a routine again by helping myself in positive ways with my social life, my body, and my mind. I began to see what I truly deserved, and it helped me make decisions as I started to love myself more and more. I regained confidence in myself, and everyone started to notice. I started to care about things such as a career and creating great relationships, and I kept the focus every day on what would make me smile.

Dani Max

I started singing again purely from feeling light in my heart and from a newfound love for my soul. I felt like a brand new person. Toward the end of my junior year, I started to see that I wanted to share with the world my passion for singing again, despite anything that anyone would tell me. Because I had moved on from my old self, I thought it was time to start new in all ways, so I created a fresh Instagram account, @DaniMaxMusic. Dani Max is my first and middle names, and I included *music* because I wanted to dedicate this new beginning to my passion and what gives me happiness, and that's music. I posted my favorite cover songs on my new page because I wanted to share my love of singing with whoever wanted to listen, which was mostly just family and friends at first.

As the summer of 2016 approached, I did another self-reflection, and I was so proud of everything I had done. I had let go of people who were abusing me, I had lost the sixty pounds that were weighing me down in more ways than one, and I started to really feel happy. Because music was a steady thing for me, I began to search summer internships in New York City to figure out if that would be my career path. Although my degree was in business, my parents encouraged me to find out if there was a different path I wanted to take instead of applying for an average business job I knew I would be unhappy with. Extremely excited, I applied to a few studios and got ready to leave college, although I would return for my senior year. I ended my junior year happier than I had been at the end of any of the other years, and with real hope for my future. I saw firsthand that I could get through anything and could do anything I put my mind to. It took such inside strength to let go of everything that had brought me down; the only thing that had been stopping me was me. I had done it, and now I looked forward to life for the first time in a long time.

When I got home for the summer, I received a call from a recording studio that creates many of the songs you hear on the radio today. When they called me in for an interview, I tried to muffle my excitement. The next day, I went into the city, wearing my coolest outfit, and met the owner, a very successful music producer. He asked me what experience I had in music, and I answered, "I really like to sing, sir." That was enough for him to let me into an extremely exclusive world, and I was so happy to have the opportunity. I was hired as an administrative assistant, which meant that I helped management with daily tasks. I was surrounded by bands, independent singers, signed singers, rappers, producers, and engineers, and I could see what life was like for people who were in the real music world. I wanted it, I wanted it all, even though I didn't know where to start. It was music talk all day every day, so it wasn't hard to find advice if I asked. When I had free time, I spoke to one of the managers about how to get a music career started, and she told me that I should create a steady social media presence with covers and then eventually create original songs. Because I had already been posting cover songs to my new Instagram account, I decided that maybe starting to write my own music was the way to go. I wasn't certain about how to do it, but one of the girls from my high school created her own music, so I reached out and met up with her. She gave me the inside scoop of how to take music seriously, and I looked up to her. She was sort of a mentor to me, even though she was just a year older. She knew everything that I was confused about, so I took her advice of reaching out to local studios.

The next time I went into my NYC studio job, I wrote my first song, "Keep That Smile," while sitting at my desk. It was a simple song of finding your own way to happiness, which was everything I had just gone through.

I went to a studio on Long Island, met with a great producer to work with, and presented my lyrics to him. We eventually created a beat that sounded more like a love song, so I decided to not use the original lyrics and instead wrote about the idea of lust when you first meet a really pretty girl. I called it "Crush." I recorded in a studio for the first time in my life, something I hadn't imagined ever seriously doing. But this was my passion, and I thought, if not now, when?

I fully engulfed myself in music and took it seriously, posting regularly and finding my niche. I realized that although anyone could listen to my songs, I wanted to direct them to people I connected with. Over time, I found that the LGBTQ+ community, people who struggle with their happiness, with loving and accepting themselves, was who I wanted to really feel my music. Being a girl singing "You can be my pretty crush" in my first song was a clear indicator that I was gay, and I knew that my words and the song would become public soon enough. I felt that it was time to be open to the rest of the world because I was fully ready to stop caring what anyone thought. Nothing was holding me back, and I was at a point where I wasn't shaken up by other people's opinions of me anymore. It was time to come out to more people I loved. I started with the rest of my family.

I sat down with my younger brother, my sister, and my grandma after a nice dinner and told them that I was gay. My brother, who was fourteen at the time, began crying. He couldn't imagine why I would ever think my siblings wouldn't love or support me because of who I chose to love. My sister and grandma felt the same way and gave me more love than I imagined. I had finally been open with all of my close family members, and now it was time to tell all of my new close friends from college.

One day during the summer I was getting off work early, and although I was shaking, I needed to just get it off my chest. There was no "right" time to just blurt it out to everyone. I called up every one of my close friends and received nothing but positive feedback from them. *This* was what friendship was, and I was so lucky to have friends and family who supported me, as I knew this was not always the case.

After being open to everyone I was with close with, I wanted to make it official in my own way, so I went to New York Gay Pride with one of my friends. Although people don't have to do this, it was something I wanted to do because I was so proud of how far I'd come. I took a picture in front of a gay flag and posted it with the caption "Proud to be me" on all of my social media accounts. At the parade, which marched all through the streets of New York City, I felt what it was like to be a part of a loving and accepting community, and I felt truly at peace with myself. I didn't care who knew and didn't want to walk around with the weight of this secret anymore. It's a constant process, even now, because people don't always know that I'm gay when they meet me. But posting it all over was my declaration to myself that I would again never hide who I was. I was finally free from being trapped inside myself. Being at Pride and coming out fully that day is a day I will never forget. I'm now able to find love with whoever I want to love. I fully embrace and accept myself, and if we ever meet, it's very possible that you'll see me wearing at least one rainbow accessory.

That summer was incredible. I created and recorded my first real song and fully came out, and now it was time to become a college senior. I was going to finish my four-year degree at a place where I had gone from my lowest point to my highest by changing my body and my mind, and I was ready to see what my positive attitude would create for me. This transformation was similar to my experience in high school, except college was the ultimate transformation for me both mentally and physically.

My junior year had been my year of letting go, and now was my time to grow and shine. I set up my dorm for the last time ever and glowed with true confidence. No one could break me of this feeling. I had great friends at school; great friends at home; felt secure, comfortable, and incredible about who I was; and was ready for my last year in college.

I continued to post my music and started using Twitter to promote my covers. I took it seriously because I loved it all. I found a recording studio in North Carolina and made a few original songs there; I had fun with it. I started to have an audience; people were following because they were drawn to my voice and message of love and happiness. I released my first song, "Grateful," to iTunes in January 2017, released "Crush" two months later, and dropped "Kiss Me Instead" a few months after that. I created weekly vlogs and "behind the scenes" and motivational videos and uploaded them to YouTube. I wanted to create them so people could understand who I was and how I became the happy girl who was singing her heart out, hoping that it would help others who were trying to feel better too. In one video, I talked about how I created my own happiness just to see what people would say, and I was blown away by the reaction from everyone who watched it. Parents, peers, and people I'd never met contacted me, letting me know how proud they were of me and how I'd inspired them. I will never forget that feeling.

Over time, I started to see that just by sharing my own experiences I was motivating people to be open, get healthy, and love themselves. People all across the world were reaching out to me, telling me how I'd helped them get through hard times or how much they appreciated everything I was doing. I heard from so many people who loved both my music and my inspiring words that I decided to turn it into more than just a hobby. These kind words showed me that we all have the power to help someone through a rough time, and I know it would have helped me when I was really sad if I knew that someone understood what I was going through. All over social media I began to speak to people, giving them advice and letting them know they are loved and are not alone. I was making more and more vlogs to explain how I'd done certain things and how they could, too.

I went through my last year of college having the most fun I'd ever had. I was happy, healthy, and free, and there was nothing I would have changed. I was having a blast with my friends, and I was creating a future I was passionate about; what's more exciting than that? I graduated High Point University with a bachelor of science degree in business administration and left as a very smiley, loving, and inspired girl. That last year, I filled my heart with love from loving myself, and I saw how many friendships I made when I opened up my heart. I am so proud of everything that college had taught me, because I ended up learning so much more than what my degree could ever teach. I really found myself. I got my life back and was now able to show other young people how they could do it too when they feel lost, sad, unloved, and unworthy.

I created my happiness from the ground up, and it took me twenty-one years to realize that positivity is a choice and that life is meant to be lived. I've grown in so many ways over the years, and I no longer recognize the old me. I've realized that happiness isn't a destination, it's something we constantly work on—because life happens. I still get upset and cry when I need to, but now I know that life is filled with opportunity, love, and excitement, and it's waiting for all of us. Things will never be perfect, but we are all here for a reason, and helping people learn to love and feel better about themselves is *my* purpose. Although every one of us has a different path, this is my journey, and I can't wait for you to share yours.

I now have a passion for helping people, and I do that in a few ways. I teach young women why they're important, why self-love is necessary, and how happiness is a choice. I share my messages through online videos, social media, and in-person conversations, and here I am now, teaching you through the published book in your hands. It is a blueprint, a resource, a guidebook to help *you* if you're feeling lost in your identity or if you're feeling unhappy and unloved.

Here we go.

Introduction

I'm here to raise you up when you don't feel good enough.

—Lyric from "Always Got You" by Dani Max

I HAVE GONE through my own experiences, taken the whole picture of what I have learned, and split them into five lessons to help you create a happy life, whatever that means for you. The first time you go through the book, I recommend following the lessons in the order that they're written. The lessons of Acknowledge, Accept, Allow, Adventure, and Activate are elements of a cycle that build on one another, and each one supports the others.

Once you understand the lessons, keep going, because the cycle doesn't stop there. To maintain your healthiest mindset and continue being happy, you have to incorporate all of these lessons into your everyday life. Happiness is something that needs your constant attention, but there's no deadline for finishing each lesson, so don't feel rushed in the process. There's also no right or wrong way to do them; it's your journey. These five lessons will help you develop a beautiful way to live, but it's up to you to take action.

Trust the process and believe in yourself, no matter how uncomfortable, messy, and difficult it can be. I've been there, so I understand. I get it. As your friend and your coach, I am here for you every step of the way. Now, let's get started on the first lesson, where you acknowledge that you're drowning in unhappiness.

XXXI

LESSON 1

Acknowledge

Happiness is key and my past won't break me.

—Lyric from "Grateful" by Dani Max

WHEN YOU'RE AT your lowest point in life or feel like you're on a downhill spiral, sometimes you don't even realize what happened or how you got there. You're so caught up in the sadness, negativity, anger, and pain that you don't stop to try to understand what led you to this moment you now find yourself in. Maybe you're feeling lost, low, or just confused with this thing called life. Maybe you're confused about who you are and why you're here. Maybe you've been taking it out on yourself by hurting yourself emotionally or physically, or even taking it out on others because of how you feel. And even when people try to help you feel better, feeling better just seems impossible. You don't understand how you can change how you feel. It just feels too big, too overwhelming. When I was self-destructive, I didn't know happiness was possible either, especially when I was drowning in my own thoughts and my own story and I didn't know how to get out.

I know you may not see it now, but you're incredible. You're strong, and you can do this. I'm proud of you for who you are, and throughout this book, you'll learn to create and live a life where you're proud of yourself, too. No matter how bad you are feeling, how sad or unhappy you are, there's a reason you picked up this book. You can even take the pressure off yourself and know that you don't even have to believe a word that I tell you, and that's perfectly okay. But, I know that if you're reading this, you're at least hopeful that a better and more

1

beautiful future is possible, even if you don't know how to get there. So keep an open mind. I've got you. This is the first lesson to creating your happiness, confidence, self-worth, and more, and it's all about acknowledging that you're unhappy.

I want to let you know a few things about my perspective of life. We are all in control of our own feelings, our happiness, and our paths. Life isn't always perfect, and situations can happen that will make even the happiest person upset . . . this is a part of life. Sometimes bad things just happen and they are nobody's fault. But even when they do happen, it doesn't mean you have to carry them with you forever. They can become a part of your story, but they don't have to be the whole story. And wherever you may be right now—lost, hurt, sad—you're not alone. It's normal to be going through things. If you feel like there is no way that life can get better, then hopefully I can help you see the brighter side of things. You picked up this book, so it's a great start.

Lastly, I've found that no matter what kind of pain you go through, you will end up okay. Over time, you will find answers to your confusion, and they may even come in unexpected ways. You may hear a song that helps you to create a different outlook, or you may try a new approach to something that helps you feel a little better. When you take action on the lessons I'm sharing here with you, you'll see that you can overcome anything, and you will be happy—as long as you keep trying. Sounds like a breath of fresh air and probably a little crazy too, right?

You see, happiness isn't easy for everyone. We're all different, and some people have to work a little harder to be happy. Everyone has their own path, so for a minute, don't compare yourself to anyone else. Let's focus on you and only you.

To be happy is a process, and it takes work. It starts with stepping back from your current mindset, taking a breath, and asking yourself, "Am I excited to wake up every day to pursue my passions and live my life to the fullest? Do I have peace in my mind and my heart for the things I can't change? Is my life the way I want to keep living it?" Ask yourself these questions, and if you answer yes to them, then put this book down, because you don't need to read it. But if you didn't automatically smile when you asked yourself if you love your life, I'm going to ask you to do something. Ready?

Be in your own thoughts for a minute, and think about your unique life in a few ways. Think about all the ways you are who you are, from your social life, work life, and school life to your family and whether you're happy with yourself as a person. I know you might be scared; I was, too. Being in your head can be one of the hardest things people do and one of the scariest places to be because it makes you look at yourself on a deeper level and there may be a lot of chaos and confusion in there. It can be difficult because so many of us are so used to doing the same thing every day, just complaining about life—or not even thinking at all. We're going through the motions, but we're numb. Just think of your daily routine: so much of it is so automatic that you might barely be thinking at all.

It's time to see what you're thinking, and I'm here to help guide you, but you have to do the work. The only way to kick off change is by reflecting on life instead of staying numb to it. Ask yourself if you're happy with your surroundings, your school, job, health, and relationships. More importantly, how is your relationship with yourself? Take time to sit with your thoughts. Do whatever you need to do to evaluate yourself and your current situation. Write it down if that helps, but get clear and be honest. And remember, no one's life is ever perfect.

When you reflect on your life, you may realize that you are unhappy in a lot of ways. That's a great first step. Acknowledging that you're truly unsatisfied gives you a place to begin; it's the start of it all. Now let's talk about your responses to reflecting on your life.

What sparks for you when you ask yourself about how your relationship is with yourself? If your answer isn't something like, "I'm incredible and I love myself just as I am," then being able to say this to yourself is the ultimate beginning. I have a secret for you, and it was the most important lesson I ever learned from my own transformation: everything in your world changes when you change your mindset and your relationship with your beautiful self. You have all the power in the world to be happy, but it starts with caring about yourself. If you want happiness, it's waiting for you. Change starts with you, but you really need to feel the motivation to be happy because no one else can hand it to you.

Now that you've acknowledged that you're unhappy, another extremely important step needs to happen: you have to be ready to make a change and then go for it no matter how scared you are. Maybe you've hit rock bottom and you're ready to create a new version of yourself, or maybe you just know you're ready to take a first step.

Sometimes, even after someone acknowledges that they don't like their life, they just keep complaining and do nothing about it. Complaining about what's wrong but never taking any steps to change keeps people doing the same exact thing over and over again. It keeps them stuck and grounds them even deeper to a negative and unhappy place.

What will set you apart from people who just stay upset their entire lives is that you are doing something about it. Find the motivation to end your old ways of thinking and being; it's the only way to leave behind the old stuff that you don't like. This decision to change needs to hit you like a ton of bricks. It needs to be the most important decision you make. It's about making a decision that you're ready to live a life filled with love and peace. You need to feel deep inside that you're ready to want the best life for yourself, no matter what. In order to change, you need to want it so bad. You need to start imagining what it would be like to smile and wake up every day excited about the moment. Hey, changing your life for the better isn't easy, but everyone has the power to take control and change. I know you have fears and doubts, but I also know that you can do this, and it starts with entering the beautiful unknown.

When I was at my lowest point, I could see that every one of my days consisted of crying and self-loathing. After years and years of having no self-esteem, no confidence, and being disgusted with my life overall, I eventually felt sick to my stomach that I had let it go that far. I thought about everything I had done that led me to that very moment, and I got so angry. I knew this wasn't the life I wanted to keep living, and that awareness hit me so hard. I felt like the oxygen was being sucked right out of me. I had no idea how to get out of feeling this way, but I had to trust myself and the universe. I was twenty years old, and the acknowledgement that I needed to change for the benefit of my mental health took over my entire body. I got an adrenaline rush, ran sobbing into my bathroom, and made the decision that I was ready to change.

So now you've acknowledged that you're sick and tired of feeling bad about yourself and your life. You fully and clearly see where you are now, and you're willing to change. Now you're ready for Lesson 2: accepting and loving yourself.

LESSON 2

Accept

Love and accepting yourself starts with you and no one else.

—Lyric from "Pride" by Dani Max

ACCEPTING AND LOVING yourself are what creates real happiness, so get ready, because this is when you will start doing things that are going to change your mindset. These two things are the main components that happiness is built on, and without them, it's hard to imagine that happiness can be achieved—they're that important.

Accepting and loving yourself go hand in hand. When you accept yourself, you understand that you sometimes can't change certain things about yourself. When you accept that you can't change certain things, you can see that those things are what make you different, and you can start to love your flaws as well as the things that make you unique. It takes time to really love and accept yourself, but when it happens, it creates a sense of worth inside of you, which helps you make better decisions.

Accepting Yourself

Accepting yourself is a big step, and it changes you in a lot of ways. It means letting go of the pain from your past, knowing what's out of your control, and being okay with who you are. It means coming to peace with your strengths, weaknesses, passions, and identity, and appreciating what you have. Acceptance does *not* mean that you accept things that you don't deserve, things like bad friends, a bad school life or job, or a bad life in general. You are worth more than that.

Accepting yourself is about being at peace with things as they are without blaming anyone else for why you live or feel the way you do. It's about being okay with who you are in this minute, even if you aren't going to the school you want, you don't have the job you want, you're not in the relationship you want, or you don't have the body or the friends you want. By accepting yourself, you can start to trust that there's a light at the end of the tunnel, and you can start to believe that things will turn around for the better. You can see that taking responsibility for your life gives you your power back and that this is what you need to do so that change can happen.

Maybe you're thinking, "What happens if I'm lost? What if I don't know all the pieces that make me unique? What if I don't know my passions, my sexuality, or what I really desire?" Everything can feel stressful when you don't know who you are, but over time, you'll start to understand who you are and what's important to you, and you'll start to create the real you.

I want you to think for a minute about what you are sure of about yourself. Maybe you're sure that you don't like math class, but there's an interesting language elective that gets you through the day. Maybe you know for sure that you love to be creative and that you don't want a career that doesn't let you be creative. Or maybe you know that you want to spend your free time with a few good friends who are honest, fun, and inspiring, people who you need to surround yourself with right now. That's a great start. Trust that you will learn over time what you want and that you will accept where you are now, because as you go through this process of learning to love and accept yourself, you will find yourself along the way.

Accepting yourself means knowing who you are and what's important to you. It means you're okay with where you are now, even if everything isn't in place. It means opening your heart up to being okay with discovering yourself whenever it happens, even if it doesn't happen when you want it to. Accepting yourself means being open to a new way of thinking and feeling without denying parts of yourself or your feelings as they begin to surface. Let's talk about *how* to accept yourself.

To help you to see yourself more clearly, write down all of your strengths, weaknesses, and passions. Write about how you feel, or if you think it would help, talk about what's going on in your life and in your head with someone you trust. Pour out everything you can think of that makes you *you*. Don't worry if you don't have all the answers yet, because you'll find them. By talking about what's going on with you, by writing about it, looking at it, and thinking about it, you'll be able to see things more clearly. You'll be able to see the cards you've been dealt in life and how and why you feel the way you do. Everything will start to make total sense once you can really see your experiences, your upbringing, and the choices you've made.

Once you see yourself more clearly, think about what has been holding you back from feeling free, happy, and incredible. Are you struggling with your past? Are you denying a piece of yourself on some level? Do you have fear or self-doubt? Are you believing someone else's opinion of you? Did you start believing an opinion of yourself that just isn't true? Are you denying your denial right now? Lots of people struggle with denial because they're afraid to uncover their true selves. To keep up their denial, they distract themselves with food, alcohol, people, TV, and other things that stop them from looking at who they are and how they really feel.

I used to not ever want to see who I was, and I sure didn't embrace myself, the good and the bad. But once I took the time to understand myself, I felt more empowered than I ever had. Wanting to deny parts of yourself that you don't like is understandable. Maybe you fear judging yourself or fear being judged by the world around you. But you are who you are, and I hate to break it to you, but running away from yourself isn't the answer. If you waste time living in fear of what you'll find, you'll only bring yourself down more, so learn to be okay with yourself.

Take a minute to think about who you are, with all of the things that make you imperfectly perfect. Dig as deep as you can. Whatever comes up will help you to find your happiness. I'm not saying it's easy, but it's necessary if you want to feel better.

Tell yourself that everything you discover about yourself during this process is okay. It's okay to have your flaws, strengths, and likes that you already have and the ones that you will find out about. It's more than okay to be who you are, because you're amazing—you're an individual put on this Earth with a real purpose, and you will find out exactly who you are when you uncover the real and deepest you. You are beautiful because of who you are and because you simply exist. It's time to understand that.

Another huge part of accepting yourself is to let go of feelings from your past. Holding on to those feelings stops you from thinking clearly and keeps you stuck in what was instead of what could be. Letting go has a lot to do with forgiveness—forgiving yourself and others. Staying angry at yourself or a situation keeps you stuck exactly where you are, so forgive yourself for any pain you're holding on to. I know it's hard. Maybe someone really hurt you and it's hard to let it go, or maybe you did something you regret and you feel a lot of shame. Be honest about all of it, and then realize that forgiving yourself sets you free. You have to let go of any resentment, anger, and hard feelings you have for what you've done or what someone did to you. Holding on to negative feelings about things you can't change won't help you in the slightest. By letting go of them, you'll come closer each day to a feeling of "it is what it is," which is the absolute healthiest mindset to be in. And with practice, you'll start believing it. Maybe those painful experiences will end up teaching you powerful lessons that can help you going forward.

To start to heal and move forward in a healthy way, spend time every day doing something that makes you feel good, go somewhere you feel supported (like a professional or someone who loves and accepts you), or meditate.

You might regret some decisions you made in the past that made you feel bad, but those decisions don't have to define you. You can't change what already happened; all you can do is learn from what happened and move forward. Like I said earlier, there aren't any mistakes in life, only lessons. This is because being imperfect is a part of life. You're only human, so give yourself a break. I learned from my lessons so I could make a better future for myself. You can, too. Find peace in your own way. This will help you heal so you can become your best self.

I've had to practice acceptance a lot of times in my life, and I'll need to again in the future. I've had times when I needed to let go of anger, I had to stop pretending to be someone I'm not, and I had to stop denying who I was. The following story is my favorite example of self-acceptance because when I accepted this piece about myself, I became freer than I ever imagined.

Remember the story I told you about when I first came out to myself, when I was seventeen? I had judged myself for years, and I'm not even sure why. I guess I was just scared. Before I accepted that I was gay, I didn't want to live a life that made anyone think differently about me, so I hid anything about myself that could be seen as different. I suffocated my feelings, pressing them down so deep in my brain that it messed with my head for a lot of years and added to my pain.

When I was younger, I knew it was normal to be unsure of my feelings because I saw that other people around me were confused, too. But as I got older, I wasn't confused anymore, I was just too scared to admit to myself that I was gay. I was in denial. I denied myself my own freedom for a long time; it was like I had locked myself in my own prison and I held the key, but I wouldn't let myself out. Finally, when my feelings became obvious to me, I couldn't keep lying to myself. I could see that it was no way to keep living. I could see that I just needed to say it, be honest, and admit it, even if I only admitted it to myself.

I began to accept this part of myself when I met that blonde-haired athletic girl, the one who was new to my high school and who I became close with and was interested in. Inside, I felt like things were deeper than friendship, and because she was openly gay, I could see the possibilities of what life being out could be like. This was the first time I experienced really accepting who I was inside. I didn't know what would come out of being honest, of accepting this part of myself and being okay with it, but I had to accept it because it was who I was, and I couldn't change it.

This acceptance made me feel free—free from the pain I caused myself, free from a future I didn't truly want. I was able to start to live a life within my own truth, and there's nothing more empowering than that.

Luckily, there are now role models all over social media talking about how important it is to be yourself. Coming out is its own process, and it's way more complex than just accepting it. I didn't have anyone to look up to when I realized I had these feelings, so I had to find it within myself to admit it, accept it, and eventually love myself as I was. Now I'm extremely proud of who I am, and my passion is to help other people come out of feeling confused, scared, and feeling like they're not okay.

Self-acceptance happens when you go through this whole process I'm teaching you, when you go through the steps of understanding, loving, and discovering yourself and continuing the process—no matter what.

Being who you are is not something to hide, and it can be easier to do when you surround you yourself with a great support system. This means friendships, support groups, and whatever helps you grow. We all need support. Sometimes it's right in front of us and available, and sometimes we need to look for it. It doesn't matter; whatever support you need and get, it'll help you accept yourself. When you accept yourself, you're one step closer to happiness. Loving yourself and embracing all the different parts of yourself is next up.

Loving Yourself

Learning how to love myself was one of the hardest things I've ever done. Before I learned this lesson, I didn't have motivation, confidence, or positive self-esteem. I was careless about myself and didn't care how I was treated because I didn't feel worthy or deserving of anything better. When I learned to love myself, everything changed.

You may not see right now that one of the reasons you're suffering is from being careless about yourself and your surroundings, but until you see it, you'll stay exactly where you are. I've learned that no matter how you look at yourself, your world is a pure reflection, a mirror, of how you feel inside, and you receive exactly what you put out. If you walk around angry and resentful, you'll get that back. If you're untrusting and cautious, you'll find evidence to confirm your beliefs. If you give off a cold or hostile vibe, you'll get that back, too.

When you don't love yourself, it shows up in a lots of ways. It shows up in how you treat yourself and how others treat you. It shows up in who you surround yourself with, how you think, dress, eat, act . . . everything. To learn to love yourself, you have to know what to keep and what to take out of your life. I know how hard it is when bad people, bad habits, and being in a bad place stop you from taking any positive steps, but when you learn to love yourself, everything changes.

Loving yourself happens when you find ways to be proud of who you are, to embrace your beautiful self, and to find your own confidence. Being able to love yourself helps you in every way possible, because when you feel good inside your heart, you are being the real you and you have more to give. When you feel better, helping yourself and others comes from a different place inside. When you feel good about yourself, you want to drop your bad habits so you can grow. Then you can be healthy mentally and physically because you respect yourself and your body. Incredible things happen when you love and accept yourself. It takes time and constant work, but it's possible. Create the habit of reminding yourself how capable, beautiful, and strong you are. Keep this habit throughout your life so you can continue to grow. Constant love for yourself creates a powerful mind and a peaceful heart, which leads to endless possibilities.

Here are a couple of ways to learn to love yourself, but the process is different for everyone. You have to see what works for you. One thing you can try is to repeat to yourself every day words like, "I'm ready to love and accept myself." This one worked great for me. Repeating a certain phrase to yourself is a helpful way to change your mindset, because you're filling your mind with love instead of hate.

When I had that total meltdown when I was twenty, my confidence and self-esteem couldn't have been any lower. The thing was, I had nowhere to turn and nobody to turn to, so I turned to myself. I finally learned that I was unhappy because I had chosen to live like that. I was sick of feeling that way, and I said, "No more!" Remember that day that I decided I'd had enough of feeling so unhappy, that day when I was crying over my sink, looking at myself in the mirror? The next thing I did was yell *"I love you, you're beautiful, and you are incredible!"* right into my own eyes. Those words were just words at the time, but I needed to hear them to begin the process of loving myself, because looking for love on the outside doesn't solve anything. I made a commitment that day that I would do this every day so I could start to change my negative thinking about myself—and it worked. It took believing in myself enough to say it the first time and to keep doing it, because the life I wanted wouldn't come without it. This was huge for me to do; I had never told myself one good thing about myself, and I didn't believe my own words at first. Eventually, I did.

Another way to learn to love yourself is to do things that you can be proud of, such as volunteering your time to your community. For example, you could help out at a community center, do something kind for someone who needs help, or do something to improve your local park or neighborhood.

Remember, loving yourself begins with accepting who you are, seeing past the imperfections, and doing something every day that you can be proud of. Remember, too, that this does not happen all at once, so don't get mad at yourself if you aren't bursting with love the first time you try to love yourself. There are a lot of benefits that come from the process, so just trust it and stay with it.

As I started loving myself, I found myself speaking out more often than I did before, and I stood up for myself—two things I'd never done before. I also began to feel more confident. I started to see that I deserved to be happy, and I didn't let anything or anyone bring me down. I stopped caring about what anyone thought of me, because at the end of the day I saw that the only opinion that mattered was my own. I could see changes in my happiness because I was taking care of my mind and my body. Because I was now loving myself, I wanted to lose weight so I could continue to feel better. I felt so much better that I began helping people because of the goodness I felt in my heart, and I loved every minute of it. When you feel good, you do good.

Being proud of who you are, having confidence and a true appreciation for yourself, come from choosing to love yourself. Learning to love yourself will be one of the greatest lessons you will ever learn, however you learn it.

When you start to work on yourself, you'll want the best for yourself, which also means taking a look at what and who you surround yourself with. For example, take a look at the people around you and the habits you have, and ask yourself if they are helping or hurting you. Once you can see these things clearly, you can move on to what you choose to allow in your life.

LESSON 3

Allow

Realized I deserved better and I can't just take whatever.

—Lyric from "Grateful" by Dani Max

LET'S DO A quick review of the first two lessons so you can see how the lesson of allowing comes in.

Acknowledge: You probably started reading this book because you are upset, lost, or angry with how your life is right now. This first thing you have to do to change anything is to acknowledge the struggles you're dealing with. This is a pretty big first step, but once it's done, you're on your way.

Accept: Once you've acknowledged what's going on, you have to decide if you want to change your life for the better. This can happen only when you make the choice from inside of you to change. Once you choose to care about yourself, when you accept and love yourself enough to realize that you don't want to be unhappy anymore, then you can see where your choices, thoughts, and feelings have gotten you where you are, and you'll be ready for something better. Once you accept and love yourself, your self-esteem and confidence grow and become a solid part of you.

Once you have acknowledged where you are and you have fully accepted yourself, you're ready to learn what you want to *allow* (and what you won't allow anymore) while you're creating your new and beautiful life.

Letting Go

You've already done the work of thinking about where your life is right now, and you've realized that some things are out of your control. But when something outside of you is tearing you down to where you feel like you're drowning and you *can* make a change, you can allow yourself to let that stuff go.

You don't have to put up with things if they aren't what you want in your life anymore. Think about your usual surroundings. If you live in a messy, dark, cluttered space, it's hard to feel good. Just organizing a bit and taking care of the space you're in gives you a subconscious message that you care about yourself. You have to let go of the negativity surrounding you so you can grow and fly, and you can start with something as simple as taking better care of your space. When you feel better in your space, you'll want to take better care of *you*.

Now let's talk about the people in your life. Nobody is perfect, and not everyone in your world is going to be glowing with happiness and ready to steer you in the right direction. But when you let the negative people in your life affect you to the point where how they act is how you act, it's time to revaluate those relationships. We accept the love we think we deserve, so when we voluntarily let someone into our lives who isn't good for us, we believe deep inside that we don't deserve people who could treat us well. It all comes back down to what we think we deserve. We become like the people who we surround ourselves with, so being around people who don't inspire or support us will never help us grow. Sometimes we can't see that someone is bad for us because we're so used to how things are that we don't even think getting out of it is a possibility.

Maybe you're in a toxic relationship that brings you down so much that you've lost sight of your own worth. Maybe you have a friend who constantly puts you down because of how they feel about themselves, and putting you down makes them feel better. Maybe a teacher, a friend, or someone you work with doesn't appreciate you, and then, because you constantly feel bad about yourself, you start to believe what they say. You will keep feeling bad about yourself as long as you allow yourself to remain around these people. It's hard to have a positive mindset if you begin to see your world as negatively as they do. Hurt people hurt people, and no matter who the negative people are in your life, they may not have a place in your future as you work toward becoming happier.

I get it that separating yourself from a toxic significant other, friend, or family member is difficult. It's one of the reasons why we put up with things a lot longer than we should. But I wasn't able to make my breakthrough until I allowed myself to let go of the negative and toxic people who were walking all over me. Negative minds feed off of others, so it makes sense that someone who is drowning would pull you down, too.

Sometimes a situation holds you back, such as someone making you feel guilty so that you stay in a relationship with them. Maybe you feel dependent on this person and don't know where to look for support. Or maybe you just love them and you're trying to heal them from their own pain, but you're getting hurt in the process. Whatever your circumstance, if you see that someone in your life is constantly bringing you down, it's time to look at what you really want. It may not be easy to drop these people from your life, but at least consider creating a safe distance from them so you can grow.

Imagine someone suffocating you and then realizing that you could stop them just by telling them to stop. Now imagine that you don't tell them to stop, and so you let them keep hurting you. This is what is happening when we let people keep hurting us. Why do we allow this? It's because we forget that our lives and our happiness are up to us and that we're in control of creating the lives we want. We put up with things we shouldn't because we don't feel worthy, or we feel insecure, or we don't love ourselves. Sometimes we just don't believe we have the strength to let go. You have the ability to tell these people to stop suffocating and hurting you, but that ability is probably buried under layers of fear, doubt, and insecurity. Don't worry; I'm going to help you find yourself under those layers.

The closer we are to people, the more they have the ability to hurt us. Someone who we barely know can't hurt us emotionally as much as someone we believe in and trust. If someone you don't know very well is going down a destructive path, you probably won't be affected as much as if it were your best friend or significant other. But when you believe in and trust someone, you assume what they're saying is true, regardless of the motivation they have behind their words. When you start to see your worth, you will be able to see how bad these people are for your happiness, but until then, you'll just accept any kind of person or behavior because that's what you believe you deserve.

I really get that the thought of letting go of someone you're close to can be stressful, painful, and even terrifying. You start imagining their response and then decide the confrontation just wouldn't be worth it. But every time you choose not to take action, you're putting your life and happiness on hold. I'm not saying it's easy. It's not. You probably can't see it now, but sometimes letting go is just what you have to do for your own health and for you to live a life of love instead of misery and pain. If you've ever let go of something that hurts you, then you how hard it was at first but then how liberating it can be.

Is there someone in your life who is putting you down, disrespecting you, or making you feel small and insignificant? There are a few ways you can discover the toxic people affecting you. You could write down the names of everyone in your life and how they make you feel. Or you can say a name to yourself and get an immediate sense of how that person makes you feel. You could think about letting go of toxic people in general, and then someone immediately comes to mind. Any one of these steps might work to identify toxic people, but you have to find your own way that works for you. It might be enough to distance yourself from certain people and their negativity. Even doing that is a big step that will let you see things more clearly while giving you some space to start making healthier decisions. I'll talk more about steps you can take to start letting go of the toxic people in your life later on.

For now, think about this. While letting go of the negative people in your life is a huge step in the right direction, you can also allow yourself to let go of other things that aren't working for you. Evaluating your life means looking at how your thinking has led to certain choices, beliefs, and results. When you see this connection clearly, you can see why you let certain people and situations into your life in the first place. Consider where you are in your life right now. Can you see how your mindset, people, location, school, friends, jobs, habits, and conditioning have led to your current situation? These things are all a huge part of our everyday lives and contribute to who we are. They are also where the choices we make can make or break us.

If you're unhappy with your weight, are you ready to make a change and have a different result? If you don't like your classes, is there an interesting extracurricular activity you could join? If you don't like your major, can you do something to switch into something that interests you? What about where you're living? Are you ready to move to a place that fits your needs, your budget, and your preferences? If you're able to make a change, what has stopped you from making it? Everyone's circumstance is different, and maybe you simply can't get out of your current situation. If that's the case, can you change how you look at it? If you want to switch your major but for some reason you can't, think about the benefits you'll get from learning about the field you're already studying. If you don't like where you live but you need to stay there for some reason, is there a way to see the good parts about living there? If you can't change your surroundings or current situation, you must change your state of mind so you can see the situation differently and see the positive that it brings into your life.

It's not always easy to let go, but it's worth it if what you're holding on to isn't working for you. Staying with someone who isn't right for you because you don't like the idea of letting go of them and of what's familiar isn't a good enough reason to stay together. Yes, that person may be familiar, but that doesn't mean they're healthy for you. It doesn't matter if it's a person, a class, a job, a place, or a habit—just because something is familiar doesn't mean it's good to keep.

To see what you want to let go of, write down some things you're willing to change. Here are some examples: To be happy while in school, drop the negative mindset if getting your degree is something you want. To improve your health, quit smoking or overeating. To improve your career, get out of your town and find new opportunities somewhere else. To be able to reach your potential, let go of a significant other who's been holding you back. You don't have to let go of everything right away, and I don't suggest that you do, but taking small steps to improve your life will lead to big results. Each change you make will show you how capable you are, how strong you are, and how much you care about yourself. Remember, letting go starts with a desire and a choice to help yourself. If you're ready, I'll show you how.

As you learned in my story, I've had to let go of lots of things in my life, and I've seen lots of people do it, too. Envisioning your future is a powerful process and the first step to creating a new life. This practice worked for me, and I hope it helps you, too. Start by imagining what your life would be like without something bringing you down. To do this, write down everything you'd like to let go of so you can see exactly what you don't want in your life right now. Once you've written your list, circle the items that you *can* let go of, then choose the one thing you'd like to let go of *first*. Now think of all the ways it would serve you to be free of this person, place, or thing. Picture what your life would look like with this change in place.

Another tip which has helped almost every person I know is to find a support system. Sometimes, when we're unhappy about certain things going on, we don't realize that there are a lot of other people in the same position we are. We think we're alone and have to figure it all out by ourselves. But we don't, and this is where support really helps. Having loving and supportive people around you is really helpful, especially when you're not feeling strong about your changes yet. Talk with a close friend, family member, coach, therapist, or a group that understands what you're going through. These people can give you the extra support and push you need to start the process of letting go, especially if they're also working on the same thing. When you are letting go of a person, lots of questions can come up, but finding the right support system helps you see that you'll be okay. You'll see that there are people out there to help you and who have been where you are now.

Earlier I talked about repeating positive words to yourself. When you fill your heart and mind with love, it feels good and you want to keep feeling this way. You help yourself in a lot of ways when you do this practice. Every day you can grow and feel happy. There are lots of resources available to learn more about letting go, becoming less attached to things that hurt you, and to be who you really want to be. For example, there are books that teach how to detach yourself from codependency, videos online, and even public speakers who talk about the importance of letting go of negativity. After you've gone through these lessons, look for other ways to create the mindset you need to keep those changes going.

When you start making changes, you will probably start getting feedback, judgment, and comments about your changes. It's easy for this stuff to derail you, but consider this: Your changes might be showing other people what they aren't willing or ready to see in themselves. By you doing something to improve your own life, you're calling them on their stuff. When you eat better, your friend sees how poorly they're eating. When you care about your schoolwork, a classmate sees how they've been severely slacking. When you're look for a new career, your coworker can see how they've been settling for a job they don't like.

It's hard for people to admit the things they don't like in their lives, so the judgment they direct at you is really about them. Just know that some people will judge you for wanting to make a change in your life, but stay committed and do it purely for you. There's no reason to feel guilty when you're helping yourself if it's what's best for you.

Here are a few examples of things I let go of that weren't make me happy. I always struggled with maintaining healthy eating habits. Over time, my bad eating habits created a version of me I didn't like or feel comfortable with, so it was time to reevaluate my habits. Bad habits can be like addictions; they're not easy to let go of. I struggled with my food habits for a long time. I used food for comfort my entire life, and that bad habit became a huge reason why I felt bad about myself. I'd gained and lost a lot of pounds many times, and I just couldn't seem to get the hang of eating in a way to keep my weight down and feel in control. I loved food and still do to this day, but it took being at rock bottom and being really unhappy to get me to finally make a permanent change.

I learned that I had to know the true intention behind wanting to let go of something. If the intention is anything other than creating a happier and healthier lifestyle, it won't be sustainable. For example, wanting to lose weight to look good for someone you're trying to impress instead of just for yourself will not be sustainable. Intentions are everything behind the real motivation to do something. I knew that every burger, bagel, and dessert I ate was pulling me further away from feeling good about myself.

Before I realized this, I didn't want to stop because I loved food more than I loved being healthy or fitting into clothes that I wanted to wear. First I had to acknowledge that this was true, then I had to accept and love myself. Once I became aware that I had an unhealthy love for food, I was able to find a desire to let go of the weight. I knew I had my family there to support me, and I had learned that I could achieve anything I put my mind to. Only then could I really let go of my unhealthy eating habits. It took time to get where I wanted to be, but when I pictured a future where I truly felt great in my own skin, it made the process much easier.

Even now, as I've maintained the weight loss, I still have days when I eat things that aren't good for me. But now that I know what it feels like to wear clothes I want to instead of wearing what fits and I've learned how unhealthy choices in the past led me to feel bad about myself, it's easier to get back on track. This new way of eating, based on self-love and feeling better about myself, prevents me from depriving myself and still allows me to feel good. I was able to let go of my unhealthy eating habits.

A friend of mine had to let go of her girlfriend who was cheating on her and not treating her correctly. In fact, I wrote a song about it called "Always Got You." When they were together, my friend wasn't happy with herself. She was looking for love of any kind, even if it meant she accepted it from someone who didn't value or appreciate her. Everyone around her told her that this girl wasn't good for her, but she didn't want to believe it because she didn't love herself and couldn't make clear judgments. She voluntarily kept someone around whose negative presence outweighed any good that was coming from their relationship. It took her a while to see that she was taking on the negative habits of this girl she was attached. After hitting rock bottom, my friend finally began to see that staying with this girl would only lead her down a path she wouldn't be proud of and that she deserved better. It took a great support system (family and friends) and knowing that she would eventually find someone right for her to be able to let go of her girlfriend. It had to be a "one and done" scenario because she knew that if she didn't cut off all contact, she wouldn't have the courage to break free. When she did let go, she felt free of the anxiety, hurt, and guilt that built up during the relationship. She didn't want to give up on someone she cared about, but she saw that she was giving up on herself by staying in the relationship. Once they broke up, she discovered the gift she gave to herself, and I could see it in her eyes. Even though she didn't realize it, this one step was a powerful one because she showed herself some self-love. It wasn't easy, but it was the start of something much better. When you're with someone because you don't want to feel guilty about being the one to break up, or if you're worried about being lonely without a relationship, it's important to learn that those aren't healthy reasons to stay together.

Sometimes you have to do difficult things in order to move forward in life, to live each day better than yesterday. Letting go of people, habits, and anything that is toxic to your well-being can be emotional, painful, and confusing. But

Coming Out Happy (Life Doesn't Have to Suck)

when holding on to something harmful, toxic, and negative hurts more than the uncertainty of letting it go, it's time to change your mindset or your surroundings. Either way, it takes true strength and a desire for something better to be able to let go. It's not easy, so if you are doing something to help yourself, you should be extremely proud. You're on your way to creating your happiness.

Now that we've talked about letting go, let's talk about letting in, about what you want to allow into your life to propel you forward.

Letting In

Throughout this book, you've learned that it takes time to feel great, and it's an incredible feeling when you get there. When you believe and understand that you are incredible and deserve nothing less, you send that message out to the world. Everything you allow into your life comes from what you believe you are worth. If you believe you are worthless, other people will view you and treat you that way. But once you love yourself enough to let go of the habits and people that hold you back, once you really see your true worth, you'll feel lighter, happier, and more powerful. You'll see that you can make any situation better, including your mindset and your surroundings. As you learn that the power is in your hands, you'll understand that you're the creator of your life. That feeling and understanding will build your confidence to keep making positive changes, growing and doing things that bring you closer to what you want.

There will always be opportunities to meet new people, go to new places, and create the changes you wish. Opportunities exist all around you, and as you feel better, you'll see that taking advantage of them is up to you. When an opportunity is presented to you, whether it's a new friend, an unexpected move, a class you're excited about, or a job offer, it's important to have a healthy mindset and good habits in place because they'll help you see things clearly. From that clear place, you'll then be able to make decisions about whether to let them into your life or not. When you're in a more healed place, the opportunities start to come in, and the choices about whether to take them on or not is entirely up to you.

Transitions, changes, and opportunities are inevitable, so knowing how to handle them when they come up is important. Changing your mindset from feeling unworthy to feeling confident and worthy will create the true understanding that you don't have to just accept something in your future if it doesn't make you happy.

What's the most important part to remember here? Once you understand that you deserve greatness, you'll make better decisions just by believing you deserve it. Be aware of your decisions, and ask yourself if allowing something in will help or hurt you.

Once you feel good, you'll want to go out and make great new friends, do some self-discovery, and take actions that help you grow. You won't be intimidated or afraid of these things but instead be excited by them. By imagining the life you want, you can see what you need to do to get there, even if you don't have all the answers yet. Taking daily steps toward creating your new life is the best gift you can give yourself. I know you can do it.

Now that you've learned about what to let go of and let into your life—what to allow—let's discuss one of the most exciting parts of your journey: adventure—discovering who you are as an individual.

LESSON 4

Adventure

There is good in all of the unknown.

—Lyric from "Be Okay" by Dani Max

WHEN YOU FIND yourself after you've been lost for some time, you go through an *adventure* in discovering who you are, inside and out. You might discover your purpose, passions, sexuality, or just what you like and dislike. This adventure is when you start to find what makes you unique, different, and special. It's a process, like all of the other lessons in this book, and the adventure can change as you change. Every time you change your mindset, you grow, whether mentally, emotionally, or spiritually. You discover things about yourself you never knew were there.

Going through a challenging time can reveal another side of you when you see how strong and capable you can be. Understanding who you are comes with time, and it changes as you do, but what's most important is that changes happen only when you are willing to reach for something better. Discoveries and adventures come from a new and improved mindset, consistent action, and growth. You must understand that only when you stop numbing and distracting yourself from what's not working and step into a mindset of "I am who I am and I'll figure it out" will you begin to make lasting change.

Self-discovery is a gift you give to yourself. It's an opportunity to see what makes you happy and to be proud of who you are and what you want. Many people get so comfortable in their everyday lives that they're practically sleepwalking through their days. They can't imagine things being any different, yet they complain that their lives aren't where they want them to be. They don't believe they can change, so they never take the time to see themselves any differently from where they are at the moment or to see what life would look like if they took an idea or dream to the next level. But you're different; you're ready to see who you really are and ready to go after what you truly want. You're ready for the adventure. So let's talk about *what* you'll discover about yourself along your journey, and then we'll talk about *how* to discover all these parts of yourself, starting with your purpose.

All over the internet, I've seen people talk about how upset they are with their lives and how they feel like they have no purpose in life. So many people don't feel like they have a purpose. They're aimlessly moving through their days without any real direction, plan, or sense of fulfillment. Sometimes it's because they don't think they're worthy of a purpose, sometimes it's because they're not *living* their purpose, and sometimes it's because they haven't figured out what their purpose is yet. This may come as a surprise, but we're all here for a reason, and every single person on the planet is here to discover and use the unique gifts they've been given. Your purpose may simply be to do what makes you happy and live a life you love because as you do, others will be impacted by your happiness. Your purpose could be anything; it's for you to discover, and I'm going to help you do that right now.

Your purpose comes from your inner core, from the deepest part of yourself. It's why you're here, what makes you unique, and what makes you the beautiful human being that you are. It's what gives your life meaning, what you're meant to do while you're here. If you haven't discovered your purpose yet, that doesn't mean it's not there. It just might be buried under layers of doubt and old habits, so trust that although you may not know what it is just yet, it's there. We aren't here just to exist, we're here to live a life of love, passion, and fulfillment, and that's how we live when we discover our purpose. This is a part of the adventure of life.

Finding your purpose isn't always easy, and in fact, you might not discover it until after you've gone through some really challenging times. Maybe you didn't have a clue about how to find the right college, so now you know you want to help others have an easier transition. Maybe you didn't grow up with healthy home-cooked meals, and now you want to be a gourmet chef. Maybe you didn't have a close family growing up, so you create a loving home with a significant other. Maybe your years of feeling alone when life threw you some curveballs made you realize you want to be a coach, counselor, or therapist.

Your purpose is what you're doing when time flies by, and it feels effortless. Whatever it is, your purpose is what makes you happy to wake up every morning, knowing you're contributing and doing what you're uniquely here to do. It's an adventure, and it's exciting to discover your purpose, and once you do, you'll be excited about all the possibilities ahead.

Once you discover your purpose, what fuels it? Let's talk about passion.

Your passion is that inner flame that gets you excited about something. It's the inspiration you feel when you get a brilliant idea, an *aha* moment, or a subconscious nudge urging you toward a choice or decision you know is right for you. Passion is the strong feeling, the deep, intuitive knowing, behind living your purpose and doing something you love. It's a feeling that fuels your soul and makes your heart happy. It's when you're excited and inspired to uniquely express your gifts with everyone around you. You can show your passion through your choice in school classes, your career path, a service you offer, a talent you have, or an action you're inspired to take. Being lucky enough to get paid for your passion is the ultimate gift. When you've combined passion with your purpose, you'll be serving at your highest level as you use your unique gifts to help others, and it'll never feel like work at all. You might not find your passion in your career, but that's okay, because your career may be what allows you to pursue your passion.

What are the benefits of living with passion? There are many, and just a few of them are reduced stress; increased confidence; a sense of accomplishment; a positive feeling from helping others; and healing yourself physically, mentally and emotionally. Every day I see people who pursue their passions through their art, the way they give back to their community through service, how intensely they play a sport, and how they teach others about something they understand and love. It all comes back to doing what you love and expressing it in your own unique way.

Take a minute to think about what makes you feel excited, happy, and empowered. Next, think about whether you are living with passion in your daily life. Are you feeling flat and dull or excited and energized? Living with passion fuels your energy better than any chemical or caffeine ever could because it gives you real energy that bubbles up from inside you.

Sexuality (LGBTQ+)

Let's talk about questioning or accepting your sexuality. Now, this piece may not apply to you, but keep reading anyway because you'll get a better understanding of what a family member, friend, or coworker may be struggling with.

I want to say here that I'm not an expert on sexuality, but as someone who struggled with herself for so long, I can give you some tips and advice from what I learned as I went through it.

Sexuality is a huge part of who you are, and being unsure can make things difficult, especially when you feel pressure from yourself or those around you. It doesn't matter if your sexuality is obvious to you or you've been battling with it for some time—wherever you are is completely okay. If you're young and confused, it's perfectly okay to acknowledge this. Maybe you're not ready to even talk about sexuality and you need to put the idea aside until you're older.

If you are struggling with understanding your sexuality, the lessons I learned and that I've talked about so far can really help you. First, *acknowledge* that you're confused about your sexuality. This was a huge first step for me, but it opened the door to everything else that followed and led me to being the confident, happy, excited person I am today. Once you've acknowledged that you're confused, follow the lesson on learning to *accept* and love yourself (over and over if you have to) so that you'll be okay with whatever you find out about your sexuality. This will prepare you to *allow* in the new opportunities that will show up, where you can discover who you really are and what makes you happy. This will take you right to *adventure*, where life really starts to open up and possibilities start to become realities. Remember, just knowing that you will eventually figure out your sexuality should help, and there's no need to label yourself before you're ready—or even at all.

Labeling myself as gay helped me understand who I was and what I liked, but everyone is different. There's no right or wrong way here. It's perfectly fine if you're trying to figure things out without labeling yourself. What held me back from understanding who I was earlier was that I was always thinking with my head instead of with my heart. I didn't even allow myself to explore, which was why I battled with myself for so long. What helped me get clear was when I had to *acknowledge* the feelings I was experiencing and how confused I was. I had to then *accept* the fact that, at the end of the day, it was okay to love whoever I wanted to because it didn't change who I was as a human being.

When I finally forced myself to let go of my fears, I let myself try new things to see what I liked, and just the fact that I stopped being afraid was so liberating. I experimented with my sexuality long enough to decide what ultimately felt right for me.

After I understood my sexuality, learning to love myself led me to feeling secure and proud with all of it. That took a long time, so don't worry if you're not clear right away. It can be frustrating when you don't have all the answers to yourself, but by accepting whatever comes and loving yourself and allowing yourself to be with whoever makes you happy, you will figure it out. Luckily, the world is becoming a more accepting place, so surrounding yourself with accepting and loving people will give you the extra push you need to feel safe in figuring out who you are and what's best for you.

A huge part of discovering your sexuality is learning that you're not alone, that there is a whole community out there of people who have been confused at some point in their lives. There are lots of resources, from influential LGBTQ+ people in media to your local LGBTQ+ community where you can understand and feel safe with being who you are. There are Pride Festivals, which are huge gatherings all over the world that help people celebrate who they are and that show how love will always win over hate. There are clothing lines promoting equality and love. People create books, articles, and movies to help society understand that for example, being gay, just like being straight, is just sexual preference and that it's okay to be with whoever you want to love.

Reach out to one of these communities or talk to someone you know and trust so you can become a part of something and find people you can connect with. Read books about sexuality or find a role model. No matter who you discover you want to be with, knowing that you're not alone is really important. It's okay to be where you are now. You don't have to have an immediate answer. This discovery, this adventure, is based on your comfort level and having the love and support of the right people. Experimenting, learning about the culture and community, and having people to talk to who have been or are in your position is so helpful, and I promise that you'll be glad you explored this important part of you.

Just as with discovering your sexuality, finding your purpose and passions are important parts of life. Get excited about the adventure of going after an opportunity to see if it's right for you. I remember hearing the saying, "You can't steer a parked car," and it's true. You don't grow when you don't take action; you grow when you try and you go out there and you find yourself. You have all the answers available to you, and life is waiting for you to live happily once you're in motion.

Besides finding the answers to huge questions such as "Why am I here?" "What fuels my soul?" and "Who do I love?" there is always room for more self-discovery, which leads to even better opportunities and adventures. This could mean finding a place you like to travel to, developing a new hobby, or tasting a new food. It all happens with being willing to learn, loving yourself, and keeping an open mind. Self-discovery, exactly like other progress I've talked about, happens when you're mindful of all the lessons you've learned so far. There can't be any self-discovery without being open and accepting yourself. It's up to you to take the time to understand yourself and to learn what makes you happy from the inside out.

When you're working on discovering and understanding yourself, you'll learn that there are no mistakes; any step you take is a step in the right direction. If you are given an opportunity and can make a choice on whether or not to take it, either choice will be okay. Why? Because even if you later think you make the wrong choice, realizing it puts you on the right path faster than anything, and you learn from it. For example, let's say you aren't sure about a college major, but you're thinking about either business or health. You decide to start with health, so you try it out and learn about the field. You eventually discover that you don't really like it and that it didn't feel natural to you, so you decide to pursue business instead. Although your first decision took some time away from your final choice, you realized that you really wanted to go into the business field because you tried out the health field. That first decision helped you see more clearly

Coming Out Happy (Life Doesn't Have to Suck)

what you did and did not want. There are no wrong moves; you will always be guided by your experiences.

Once you're in the discovery and adventure phase, take opportunities as they present themselves, just like you learned in Lesson 3, Allow. New connections with people and experiences can lead to endless new opportunities, and you can never know where these connections can lead you in your self-discovery. Trust your gut and trust the universe; you'll figure yourself out, and remember to enjoy the adventures along the way.

With that, let's move on to the last lesson, where you will activate your mind with your new knowledge.

LESSON 5

Activate

You will be okay. So take all of your fears and doubts and let them fade away.

—Lyric from "Be Okay" by Dani Max

THIS IS THE last piece of the cycle of getting out of any bad place you might be in and creating something new and healthy. Be sure to keep all of the lessons so far at the front of your mind to help you grow and maintain your highest and happiest self.

By now you understand the cycle of what you need to do to *start* loving yourself and your life, but the cycle isn't finished yet. This will keep you moving toward living the life you want. This last lesson is about activating a steady mindset that is built on all of the other lessons. This is the lesson that will teach you how to keep those other lessons going so you can maintain the mindset you've been working on and have it become a natural part of who you are and how you think.

You've seen how important your mindset is. It's at the root of your thoughts, actions, beliefs, behaviors, responses, and reactions. Your mindset creates who you are and why you see things the way you do. Once you've created a mindset that will move you toward where you want to go, it's important that you keep strengthening it so it becomes a natural way to think and feel. This is how you will stay inspired; keep growing; and stay confident, happy, and excited about what the future holds.

Picture this great life you're creating as a wheel. Your knowledge, experiences, and visions for yourself are all inside the wheel, but without something to give the wheel a push so it can gain momentum and speed—to activate it—it'll just stay still. You have the power to use all of the lessons you've learned here to create a happier and more purposeful life, and now you can set the wheel in motion in order to get it rolling and keep it going. The wheel will need your constant monitoring and attention until it gains momentum and starts moving on its own. I talked about how you need to find the motivation and inspiration inside of you to take action when you're unhappy and have been just settling for living a life you don't want. When your mindset is activated and you're motivated to strive for something better, you'll have the momentum to create the life you want most.

It's important for you to know that you are a warrior. How do I know you're a warrior? You never would have picked up this book, let alone made it this far, if you hadn't been ready for a better life. You're aware you're not playing full out, living in a body you want, enjoying the relationships you'd like, or spending your days in a way that makes you feel happy and fulfilled. You see it's time to move through your old habits and make changes, and with time, awareness, and your new growth-minded mindset, you will receive everything you really deserve.

From this moment on, commit to doing everything with heart, passion, and desire until you achieve what you want. You must be your number one fan and best friend to yourself, because if you don't believe in yourself, no one else will. You must keep believing, *especially* when it's easy not to, because that's what will keep you moving forward. Look at it like this. The stronger you feel pulled to go back to your old ways and the harder it gets to keep moving forward, the more you can show the universe how serious and committed you are. Each obstacle is like a little test, showing you and others how much you really want to change.

There's a saying, "The road to mediocrity is a crowded one," and this is because most people are okay living without questioning anything. You're on a different path now, and it's going to take you somewhere much better than you ever thought possible. Just keep going, never give up or give in, and before you know it, you'll accomplish whatever it is you want to, despite what life throws at you. Even if you're reading this book and still don't believe how strong you are now, trust the process. Everything will eventually make sense if you follow these lessons at your own pace. You are more capable that you know.

Besides believing in yourself, another key to keeping your motivation high is to appreciate yourself during every step you're taking along the way. Appreciating yourself is different from loving yourself. Appreciating yourself comes from seeing the road you've traveled, the changes you're now making, and recognizing and acknowledging the steps you're taking to get here. It's when you're thinking about and understanding your past, thinking about what you've overcome and why you deserve to be proud of your strength. It's important to appreciate everything you've accomplished along the way—even the failed attempts. Every one of those attempts shows how you tried and didn't give up.

Think about it. Why are we so hard on ourselves when we try once or twice and we don't succeed? We didn't do that when we were babies. When we were young, we saw other people walking and we wanted to do that, too. We crawled, then stood, and then probably fell down. We tried again and again and again until we were walking like everyone else. Did we get down on ourselves for falling? Of course not. Every time we fell, we simply tried again. Same thing here. Be proud of every attempt you make toward creating better habits that will lead to a better life for you. Eventually, you'll get the hang of what's working and how to keep it going, just like you did when you were learning to walk.

I really want to stress how important it is that it's okay to fall. The only real failure is when you give up on yourself completely. Every failed attempt just means you need to find another way to make it work, and every time you try again, you're making your will, determination, strength, and resilience stronger. Just because you come out of a really bad place doesn't mean you won't be tested again; in fact, this is when you get to use your new skills to go about things differently. You will get upset, and you will get hurt—it's inevitable. But a positive mindset will eventually bring you back up from feeling bad. Those disappointments then become an opportunity for you to see how much you've grown since your last disappointment. When you know that things happen just because they happen, when you don't take them personally or use them as excuses to give up, you will see how strong you are in dealing at whatever life throws at you.

Lots of people have a setback and then look to numb or distract themselves to avoid it instead of working through it. But *not you*, so don't be hard on yourself if you're not feeling strong every moment of every day. It's okay to not be okay,

Coming Out Happy (Life Doesn't Have to Suck)

and as these moments come, you must deal with them in order to get through them. You have to deal with your emotions, not run from them, in order to heal from anything. You can't just distract yourself with the outside world when you feel upset, because then you stop looking internally and will never fix a problem.

Remember not to compare yourself to anyone else. You have no idea where they're coming from or the story behind their journey, so just keep moving forward on your new path. Processes like journaling, meditating, centering yourself, and just taking time to think will help you recognize and appreciate how far you've come.

When something is making me upset, even now, after my personal transformation, I can see that how I handle any situation is up to me. I can sit in misery, or I can try to feel better. Every time I slip, I see that happiness has a way of finding me because I look for it. I don't ever want to be as sad as I used to be, so I use these lessons to get me back on track when I stumble. It's all about the mindset I've created by reading books like these, finding the strength within myself, and understanding that having a great life or a miserable life is totally up to me.

When I get sad, angry, or upset about something, I don't numb or distract myself from it. I give myself time to be upset, then I tell myself the loving and inspiring words I need to hear to help me get through it. I still go through the process of understanding and *acknowledging* what I'm upset about. If it's something I can change, I go through the cycle of lessons by next *accepting* how I feel and loving myself enough to make a change when I'm ready. I then *allow* myself to let go of what is upsetting me. Then I'm ready for the *adventure* that comes from making a change. My mindset is always *activated* because I always pay attention to it, so I always end up making a change. I end up making a change because I believe in myself. I've overcome things before, and I know I can do it again. If something happens that is completely out of my control, such as a death, I tell myself that I will be okay in time, because I will *always* be okay. I tell myself how strong I am, and now I believe it because I've been filling my mind and my life with positive words and action. I've seen that any situation can be handled, that we are never victims who must sit and stay in misery.

To maintain steady progress toward your new and best self, keep your mindset activated by going through this book again and repeating the lessons you've learned here. Remember that this cycle doesn't end. Each time you run through the lessons, you'll see new things that aren't working, you'll appreciate how far you've come, you'll see the changes you've made that are now healthy habits, and you'll be able to get through the hard times more successfully. There's no finish line here.

These lessons worked for me, and I know they'll work for you, too. You're on a journey to your best self, and as you grow, new situations and scenarios will show up as opportunities for you to continue to grow. You've woken up and become aware that creating your best life is up to you. It's an exciting road ahead full of adventure and discovery.

Life will never be perfect, but it's all about how you choose to handle yourself, your emotions, and your path. Your future can be incredible, you can achieve happiness, and by creating and maintaining a positive mindset, you truly can do anything. It's your life we're talking about here, so do whatever it takes to create and keep that new mindset in place. Take your happiness seriously, and do what you need to in order to make yourself happy. Go after all of the exciting possibilities in life, even though you can't guarantee the outcome, and never ever give up on yourself. You're worth so much more than that. You'll never know how great you are unless you try, unless you believe enough in yourself to keep going even when it seems crazy and impossible or the people around you are pressuring you to stop. It's the crazy ones who change the world, and it was the ones who told them they were crazy who were left behind. I believe in you, and it's time you do, too. Activate your key to happiness, and it's yours to keep. You got this.

Epilogue

Best friend I always got you.

—Lyric from "Always Got You" by Dani Max

You've seen throughout this book that happiness is a choice. You are the creator of your own life, and you have the power to change the things that aren't working for you. If you are confused and tired of being upset like I used to be, make the effort to work through all five of the lessons, in order, the first time you try to make changes, and you will feel better. You'll become stronger, happier, and more fulfilled by working these lessons into your daily routine, and then you'll see how useful it is to keep practicing the cycle in your everyday life.

These lessons will bring you back up when you feel like you're slipping, losing momentum, out of place, lost, or unhappy. Happiness is a state of mind and a state of being, but it may not come naturally to you because of what you've been through or what you've believed up until now. Your mindset toward happiness is something to keep strengthening, just like a muscle. It's never a destination but a way of life. Understanding and practicing these key lessons will help you transform your entire life, heal what is broken, and allow you to live as the amazing person you're meant to be. I know how being happy can change you at the core. I know it's what you deserve and something worth working for. I hope some of these lessons have helped you already, and I'm so happy you took the time to read this book.

Here's a recap of what I learned and what I hope you have, too: These are five life lessons to finding your true happiness. First, you have to **acknowledge**. This happens when you see clearly that something is bothering you, which leads to a spark inside of you that becomes aware and ready to make a change. Next, you must **accept**. Accept yourself with all of the flaws and strengths within you, and then you can eventually love yourself for everything that makes you unique. Self-acceptance and love build self-worth and confidence, which leads to better decisions and a true peace within yourself. Then you begin to **allow**. Allowing is about letting go and letting in. It's about recognizing when it's time to let go of what's hurting you and exchanging it for what's good for you and what helps you heal and grow. You are affected by your surroundings more than you may realize, so letting go of negativity and letting in positive people, habits, and surroundings is crucial for your growth. Life starts to really change and become about the **adventure**. This is when you actively try to discover your purpose, passions, likes, dislikes, sexuality, and more. You become open to all the possibilities of what you may find about yourself, and when you do figure out who you are, you feel great about being honest with yourself. It's liberating to know who you really are, and the more comfortable you are with yourself, the more confidence and self-esteem you have. You're not trying to be like anyone else, to fit in or hide what makes you who you are. You're *celebrating* your uniqueness, because there's no one else like you. Then you're ready to **activate**. Now you're ready to create and activate a mindset built on all of the lessons you've learned to keep you on track and motivated during this exciting journey. Your mindset creates your perception of how the world, the decisions you make, and the path you take, so keeping a healthy mindset and your new, healthy habits in place is key to creating the life you want.

I know this journey isn't easy, but think about the reward. You're giving yourself the gift of happiness, and that's better than any other present you could possibly give yourself. Happiness is the base that all great things grow from. It's the fertile soil that helps all greatness grow.

The way to self-awareness and realizing that you are capable of changing your life is now in your hands. I'm so proud of you for taking the first step by reading this book. As your coach, friend, and someone who's been there, I'm rooting you on every step of the way.

I love hearing stories about how people have been impacted by my words and how they use them to help themselves, so if you were inspired to make a change, I'd love to hear from you! Please reach out and share your story with me. I know you can create anything you want, and I'd love to hear about your successes as a result of something this book inspired within you.

To contact me, see updates, current projects, and connect on social media, please go to DaniMaxWorldwide.com.

You are not alone in this world. You are strong, incredible, and loved. Believe that, and you're halfway there. You are able to transform your life, and it all starts when you're ready. I love you, and it's time to show yourself the love you deserve, too.

To your happiness,
Dani Max

About the Author

Dani Max has become an influential figure to many young adults because of her personal transformation at an early age. She is a twenty-two-year-old Certified Life Coach, entrepreneur, author of two books, singer/songwriter, and LGBTQ+ advocate. Her music helps people overcome their personal battles, and her workshops, speaking events, products, and coaching programs are all designed to help young people with their self-esteem, happiness, and identity. Dani recently graduated from High Point University. She lives on Long Island, New York, and hopes to continue inspiring the world, one person at a time.

Dani Max
Find out more at DaniMaxWorldwide.com
To connect with Dani:
DaniMaxMusic.com
Instagram/Twitter: @DaniMaxMusic
iTunes/Spotify : Search Dani Max
Facebook: Facebook.com/danimaxmusic

Made in the USA
Middletown, DE
21 September 2017